*YOUR KEY TO SUCCESSFUL WRITING*

*By the same author:*

THE ART OF DRAMATIC WRITING

# Your Key
# to Successful Writing

*by* LAJOS EGRI

*A handbook for the layman who
wants to write, and for the writer who
wants to understand the layman.*

HENRY HOLT AND COMPANY
NEW YORK

FIRST EDITION

For: *Charles, Ruth,* and *Ted*

# Contents

# Contents

CONTENTS

# *Note*

*This book is the natural sequence to my original one,* The Art of Dramatic Writing. *The letters I have received from all over the world have convinced me that I am on the right road and I can confidently try to break deeper into the uncharted wilderness of writing.*

*In my first book I was concerned mostly with the basic principles of writing and I had neither space nor time to show how to apply them.*

*I repeat the same principles here in abbreviated form as a guide for new readers.*

*YOUR KEY TO SUCCESSFUL WRITING*

# CHAPTER 1

# What This Book Says

A STORY or play can easily be as sick as a human being. Lucky—and rare—is the writer who can diagnose his own work. If a story or play lacks healthy red blood, suspense, it also lacks life.

Lack of suspense actually means that you have no living characters in your story or play. Real people with whom we can identify ourselves are interesting, especially when they are in trouble—or when they are about to make a momentous decision.

Half-realized characters do not carry conviction and consequently can't ever hold our interest, arouse our sympathies, or create suspense.

Suspense is the result and not the origin of conflict.

All great fiction writing is great because suspense, that all-enduring substance, is present in it. Only suspense has the magic power to transform a work of fiction into a living and immortal piece of writing.

How can one achieve this desirable attribute?

What is the secret? Perhaps there is a trick that one can learn in a hurry?

Yes, there is something to learn—but not in a hurry. Suspense is genuine interest in and fear for people we know to be in distress. The great secret, then, is to create characters we can recognize as people we know.

This statement is so simple and at the same time so complicated. Shall we write about our fathers, mothers, relatives, friends, and acquaintances? We know them best, all right, but how should we expect that someone in Cambodia will know them too?

If you know those relatives and friends of yours as you think you do and describe them to the best of your ability and if your picture is true to life, a miraculous thing will happen. People in Cambodia, in Africa, in Australia, and on all parts of the globe will claim that the person you wrote about is actually someone they know intimately.

You see, people are the same all over the world. The difference is only the difference between individuals.

This book shows how we can realize lifelike human beings—and without committing arson or mayhem create suspense, the life blood of all writing.

# CHAPTER 2

# I Accuse

THE FOLLOWING discussion should interest those countless unknowns who wish to be writers.

Why?

Because there are people—including writers and playwrights—who claim that creative writing cannot be taught. A strange claim indeed! Since I am doing just that—teaching what can't be taught—I feel some kind of explanation is in order.

Everything under the sun is being taught, so why not writing? What are the insurmountable obstacles that make teaching creative writing impossible?

Must one be born a genius in order to become a writer? Not necessarily. The fact is, no one who claims that writing can't be taught is a genius. Far from it!

Let me ask once more: Can one teach creative writing?

My answer is: Positively *yes*! I know too well that this statement is in direct contradiction to the belief of many who occupy important positions in the academic and theatrical worlds. Their denial of the obvious is a sad commentary on their own limited grasp of the subject.

[3]

I, for one, agree wholeheartedly that a person who lacks:
1. *Intelligence*
2. *Imagination*
3. *Honesty*
4. *Humility*

cannot be a writer.

Intelligence is the capacity to observe, to learn, and *the ability to apply what you have learned.*

Imagination is to a writer what wings are to a bird.

Honesty should be truthfulness to the point of pain.

Humility is the sum total of intelligence, which ends in wisdom. Without humility you become blind and are unable to see your fellow man.

Now, if the dissenters mean that you can't teach a person who has no ability, I gladly agree. Can every boy in the United States become a great athlete? Of course not. He'd have to possess a fine body to start with, plus an unbounded enthusiasm for his particular sport.

Any young man or woman who has the experience, intelligence, and imagination (in short, everything that is necessary for successful writing) positively can be taught the fundamentals of writing. Our scholars nevertheless shrug their collective shoulders complacently and say in chorus: "It can't be taught. All this one must learn by himself."

That is not true. It *can* be taught—and *must* be taught—to those who are not only willing but ready to do anything to realize their dreams of becoming writers.

It is simple logic that not even a Raphael or a Michelangelo can teach a blind person to paint. Nor could Paganini teach a deaf person to play the violin. No Pavlova or Nijinsky can teach a legless person to dance. Not even Shakespeare, nor Molière, could teach writing to one who lacks intelligence, imagination, or sympathy for his fellow man.

All this is painfully obvious. No one can be a writer without intelligence and an overdose of perseverance besides.

I wonder if you are aware of the salient fact that even geniuses fail more often than they succeed—for the simple reason that they had no one to help them.

Anyone who has the above-mentioned four characteristics can become a writer, a painter, a dancer, a musician, if he really wishes to. No doubt it will be a hard road to travel, but who can stop a visionary if his heart is set on a goal?

I am afraid all this "can't teach" chorus springs from people who have achieved some degree of success and who now think they are the privileged, the chosen ones of the Muse. What they know is rare, inborn—so it can't be taught!

I accuse these people of senseless double talk and short-sightedness. They are the false prophets of the theater. Instead of helping the new generation, they actually retard the development of new playwrights.

The possibility of learning is endless. Let the people who don't believe in teaching step aside and stop discouraging those having strength, vision, and hope for a new and vigorous theater of tomorrow.

CHAPTER 3

# The Basic
# Principles of Writing

FOLLOWING is a list of the basic principles of writing. In later chapters most of these subjects will be enlarged upon and illustrated with examples.

It is imperative that every type of writing should contain the following:

Premise
Pivotal character or characters
Character (three-dimensional)
Unity of opposites
Growth
Orchestration
Point of attack
Conflict
Transition
Crisis
Climax
Resolution

These twelve parts are as indispensable in writing as are the vital organs to the human body.

## Premise

The premise is the seed from which the story grows. The premise is the thumbnail synopsis of the story or play you wish to write.

It isn't compulsory but it is wise to formulate your premise first. You might have an idea or have read or heard something that seems to constitute a good story idea. No matter where your inspiration comes from, you must know exactly what you want to say, why you want to say it, and how far you want to carry it.

If your story pertains to greediness, to which you are opposed, you'll want to know in what direction and how far you intend to go with this idea, what will be its final resolution. This crystallization of your story is the premise.

You might want to say: "Greediness leads to destruction," or "Greediness leads to humiliation," or "Greediness leads to isolation," or "Greediness leads to loss of love." You can go on indefinitely, formulating premises for yourself, but when you decide on *one,* capture the one which expresses *your* idea perfectly. Then you have your story in a nutshell.

The premise should include the basic facts about the *character, conflict,* and *resolution.* For instance, "Honesty is the best policy" is not the best premise. We see the character, an honest person. But where is the conflict? This person is honest all through life and all through the play; he's very happy, nobody bothers him. A wonderful life— but a very bad play. But—if we use a premise, "Honesty defeats duplicity,"—we know immediately that our honest

[7]

person is going to engage in conflict with a dishonest person. There is inherent drama in this premise.

In short, the first part of any premise should represent character: honesty, dishonesty, selfishness, ruthlessness, false pride, etc. The second part should represent conflict: "Dishonesty leads to exposure," "Ruthless ambition leads to destruction," etc. The third part should represent the resolution or goal of the play or story.

As we see, a good premise is an indispensable part of good writing. A premise is a goal.

Many so-called scholars ridicule the idea of working out a premise before starting to write a play or story. They state that great stories were written before anyone knew anything about premises. This is true. But it is also true that even the greatest writers wrote more bad plays or stories than good ones. Without direction (a premise) they floundered!

When one intends to drive a car from New York to San Francisco, he usually uses a road map for more direct routes and good roads. The premise is the road map for all kinds of writing.

The next thing we ask is, who is going to carry out the author's premise. The characters?

Let's see if this is true. Let us suppose that we are intrigued by a braggart. We want to write about him. He claims that he comes from excellent stock, knows the best people, knows everything, in fact. He earns a lot of money, has the greatest hope for the future, and, according to him, he's the greatest guy he knows.

Naturally not a word of this is true. You're justified in asking, "Why all the bluff?" The answer is, this poor fellow really has nothing whatsoever to boast about, so he concocts these grand and glorious lies. Bluffers, liars, boasters usually do this sort of thing to cover up their physical or mental inadequacies.

Now, how can this story end? Failure and humiliation for this character seem obvious. So if you're going to write a story about such a character, don't you think it is wise to know in advance how he's going to end up?

If you know the end of your story before you start to write it, you are in a better position to write a good one. Find out who your character is, where he comes from, why he is a failure. Because it's his failure he's trying to cover up with his lying. If you have this advance knowledge, you are in a better position to do a more thorough job.

For such a story I think the premise should be: "Bragging leads to humiliation." This play or story can be a drama, satire, or both, but never a comedy. However, you can make a fine comedy out of the bragging idea if you change your premise to read like this: "Bragging leads to success." Read *The Show Off* by George Kelly. It is a satirical comedy written on the above premise.

You'll do better if you try to crystallize whatever you want to say and find your premise before you begin to write.

### Pivotal Character

Now, who is going to force the characters into action. The honest person may never be troubled by his dishonest friend (to quote our first premise) unless one of the characters forces the issue and in so doing creates conflict. This person would be called the pivotal character. The pivotal character forces the conflict from beginning to end in play, story, or novel. The other characters may be uncertain as to what they want or where they want to go, but the pivotal character knows immediately what he wants.

[9]

A selfish person is selfish when the play opens. He is *relentlessly selfish*. The pivotal character is always relentless. A pivotal character is not motivated by a whim. He has a duty to perform. He must force the conflict to the bitter end, never backing down in the middle of the play or story.

He is relentless because circumstances beyond his control force him to be relentless. If an honest man steals, it is not for the thrill or luxury of it. It is because his family is starving, or perhaps because there is illness present. This pressing need for money is a matter of life or death. A man can murder because of a ruthless ambition, desire for revenge, frustration, etc. But whatever the reason, it must be a relentless one.

When the pivotal character stops forcing the conflict, the story ceases too.

The pivotal character usually wishes change. He's dissatisfied. He is militant, ruthlessly militant, whether fighting *for* or *against* his *status quo*.

The pivotal character is the motivating power; he's the cause of conflict in your story or play. If he's ambitious, he won't hesitate to commit blackmail. He must be cunning and ruthless and if necessary ready to commit murder in order to achieve his goal, whether this goal is for good or for evil. If he's a good pivotal character, he holds nothing sacred and feels that nothing can stop him from reaching his goal.

If a writer doesn't understand the mechanism of a pivotal character, he won't know in what direction his story is going. The pivotal character knows where he's going, and tries to force everyone to go his way. If the antagonist refuses to go along with him, it's not because the pivotal character didn't push him hard enough. The pivotal character is a stubborn individual who sees only his own goal.

The pivotal character is the heart of all stories, pumping in all the conflict. If he stops pumping, your story or play stops living, just as your body would stop living if the blood stream were cut off.

I wonder if you can define the difference between a conservative and a reactionary?

The conservative is satisfied with himself, his country, and the world as they are and wishes to keep them that way; but he's too busy or too lazy to fight for this principle. He feels that everything will come out all right in the end.

The reactionary, on the other hand, wishes to keep his life and everything else as is, like the conservative, except that he will go all out to fight for his principle, and if necessary will die for it.

The difference between a liberal and a radical is the same. The former feels that the world needs a change, but hopes that somehow things will work themselves out in the long run.

The radical, however, instead of wishing or waiting, goes all out and fights for what he sincerely believes in.

The pivotal character is always on the side of the militant. He is militancy personified. Only great passion makes pivotal characters.

Here are a few examples of pivotal characters:

He wants to take *revenge* on the man who ran away with his wife.

He wants to take *revenge* on the man who sent him to prison on a trumped-up charge and took his business away.

He wants to take *revenge* on the man who ruined his daughter and refused to marry her.

He *loves* a woman madly but he must make money first to marry her.

He is willing to *give* his life for his country which he loves more than anything in this world.

He is willing to be a martyr for his religious belief.

He is greedy. His greediness sprang from poverty and now he ruthlessly exploits others for fear of hunger.

He is ready to destroy others to achieve his goal.

He may want to be a musician, or a scientist, or a dancer, or an inventor, etc.

Great men are usually outstanding pivotal characters; great criminals belong also in the same category.

## Character

The third important factor in writing a story is to look for "character." Who are these people? Where do they come from? What was their childhood like? What is their background? What are their plans in life? their dreams, hopes, ambitions, frustrations, and complexes?

Character is the vital material with which an author must work. Thus, he must know this subject thoroughly.

Every object has three dimensions: depth, height, and width.

Human beings have three additional dimensions: physiology, sociology, and psychology.

It is not enough to know that a man is rude, polite, religious, atheistic, moral, or degenerate. We must know why. Why is he any of these things? Why is his character constantly changing, and why must it change whether he wants it to or not?

The first dimension, the physical, covers the appearance and general health of the character. A healthy person reacts differently to things than an unhealthy one. Health makes the difference in his attitude toward life. It may make him tolerant or humble, defiant or arrogant. It affects his mental development, resulting in either an inferiority or a superiority complex.

The general idea that beautiful women are dumb has its foundation in the fact that life has been made easier for them. People are supposed to cater more to beautiful individuals, men or women, which means that they have to exert less ingenuity to attain any object in their favor. A less attractive woman has to work hard for her achievement or accomplishment, which in turn sharpens her mind and molds her into a better person.

The sociology of the character is the second dimension. There is a vast and obvious difference between children born in the slums and those born in the lap of luxury.

Environment means home life, marital status of parents, earning power, whether divorced, widowed, compatible, or incompatible. How did the character's friends affect him and how did he affect them. What schooling did he have? What was his attitude in school, his favorite subjects, his special aptitudes? What kind of social life did he lead?

The third dimension, the psychological, is the result of the previous two dimensions. This third dimension will give life to ambitions, frustrations, temperaments, attitudes, and complexes of the character.

To understand the actions of an individual we must first find their motivation.

Does a man have large ears, bulging eyes, long hairy arms? Does he dislike talking about crooked noses, large mouths, thick lips, and large feet? Perhaps he does, because he has one of these defects. One person may resign himself to physical handicaps, another pokes fun at them, while a third may be resentful. Many people do not escape the effects of a particular shortcoming. You must know your characters even better than you know yourself.

### Unity of Opposites

In a good play each character must serve a purpose. He should be an integral part of the whole structure so that if he is removed, the structure collapses.

How can the author integrate each and every character he selects? Simply by creating a bond between the characters or what is known as a unity of opposites. These people might oppose one another, but they cannot walk out on each other, because they are united by a common bond. However, when certain character traits are broken or changed, there is an out.

A wife hates her husband. Why doesn't she divorce him? First, because they have children; second, she is dependent upon him financially. Usually children alone cannot bind the characters together, except when there is an extraordinary love for them. There must be something greater at stake. For instance, money, business, honor, revenge, threatened murder, blackmail, etc.

For our unity of opposites we ask this question: What is the unbreakable bond between the characters? What is so much at stake that they cannot leave each other?

In Hemingway's "The Killers," the unrelenting search for the man they are to kill constitutes the unbreakable bond.

In Maupassant's "The Necklace," vanity is an excellent unity of opposites.

In Jack London's "Making a Fire," the unbreakable bond is the freezing cold against the man's hopeless struggle to live.

In Betty Smith's *A Tree Grows in Brooklyn,* the mother's unselfish devotion to her children constitutes the necessary bond.

In *Hamlet* it was revenge for the father's death.

In *Othello* it was Iago's determination to revenge himself on Othello.

In *A Doll's House* it was Nora's love for her children and her financial dependency upon her husband. (In Ibsen's time women did not work.)

In *Romeo and Juliet* it was the title characters' deathless love for each other.

Love, ordinary love, cannot be a good unity of opposites. The love must be great, deep, and death-defying if it is to serve as a strong enough bond. Let us assume the premise of a story to be, "Possessive love leads to isolation." The pivotal character would be the selfish person. Let's make her a mother who, under the pretense of sacrifice, tries to ruin her children's lives. She tries to separate them from their spouses because she's jealous of them. She demands her children's constant attention. Her children are bound to her because of loyalty, love, pity (she might be ill or financially dependent upon them), or because they are in the habit of obeying her every whim.

Breaking the bond would come when the children's love has turned to disgust, disillusionment, and loss of loyalty. They would finally see through their self-sacrificing mother and leave her all alone, stranded. This is the premise of *The Silver Cord*.

## Growth

Everyone needs nourishment in order to grow. In order to have growth in writing, we must feed it with conflict. Conflict results from contradiction. Contradiction is the outgrowth of two strong wills, desperately straining against each other. Desperation is an empty phrase unless we understand that it springs from hopelessness.

Frustration grows from disappointment. A tiny bit of frustration might grow into tragedy.

Again, conflict is contradiction. Contradiction, animosity, fear, jealousy, covetousness, hate, and ruthless ambition. These are the ingredients upon which conflict thrives. Just as a person cannot live without sustenance, conflict cannot grow and thrive without our feeding it with troubles and miseries.

It is the duty of the writer to feed these human passions generously, if he would later have them work for him.

In attempting to rectify one wrong decision we commit another, then commit a third to rectify the second, ad infinitum. Some persons will concede defeat in time to prevent destruction. Others who are stubborn and tenacious will never give up. They'll defy pressing circumstances. They'll carry on against all the laws of organized society.

So, for the express purpose of drama, a writer should be interested only in characters who, by their physical and environmental make-up, are predestined to attempt to cut through life like the ancient who cut the Gordian knot with a sword. These characters are reckless people. They burn with a holy zeal. They try to achieve their goal, no matter what the price. However, these ruthless people become desperate *only after dire necessity* forces them to a decision and any delay in acting might cost them their lives, wealth, health, or honor. Desperate necessity propels these characters toward their ultimate goal, clearly stated in the original premise. Thus, every living character grows only through conflict.

Persons grow and change every second of their lives. Some people grow rapidly, others more slowly. Husbands and wives living together for years may change so gradually it will hardly be noticeable to themselves. But a person who has not seen them for years will be startled by the perceptible changes.

Drama is not life itself, but the essence of life. Within the space of two hours' time, we must see tremendous growth in characters. The greater the conflict in human life, the faster and more apparent the growth. Since on the stage a lifetime must be condensed into two hours, the changes must be great.

In a novel, the growth is more measured. The author can take his time. He can follow his characters through the years to the end of their days. However, the characters must still grow. For instance, a selfish person might grow to be generous, a jealous person become distrustful, a disloyal person turn loyal. This pole-to-pole growth and how it happens makes the most exciting story in any form.

## Orchestration

It is a truism that everything has its opposite. There is no light without a shadow; life is a contradiction to death. Opposition or contradiction exist even in the stars, where an invisible adhesive power called gravitation prevents our pitifully small earth from being smashed into pieces. The same law governs the invisible atom, where the positron exerts the unifying force amid the positive and negative electrons and protons, while they pull and push each other around like mad dervishes.

Contradiction, the basic principle of life, is manifest also in the creation of the arts. The compositions of the dance are unthinkable without contradiction in movement. The same holds true in painting, where opposing lines

[ 17 ]

and colors create a desired unity. In music, harmony cannot exist without disharmony.

The same law governs all writing. Contradictory characters pitted against one another, such as naïve against worldly-wise, evil against just, clash while the all-powerful premise, the equivalent of the positron in the atom, will be the unifying force which will drive the contradictory characters toward their predestined ends. When contradictory characters are unified by the premise, we have orchestration.

Without good orchestration, no intelligent composition is possible. We have to be alert and find contradictions everywhere. If we fail to find them, it will not be because they do not exist, but because we failed.

Is there such a thing as injustice? Yes, there is. If you do something against me, that act is unjust. If I do something against you, that act is just. Apparently a third force must exist like the positron and the sun in this case, a judge, to coordinate this seemingly unharmonious contradiction.

If there weren't any force to control these contradictions, life would not be possible.

Let us say once again that contradiction is everywhere and in all of us. Nora in *A Doll's House* is naïve, her husband Helmer is worldly-wise.

All good plays, novels, and short stories are based on the same principles:

| | |
|---|---|
| Honesty | Dishonesty |
| Conventionality | Unconventionality |
| Morality | Immorality |
| Generosity | Miserliness |
| Impractability | Reality |
| Superstition | Science |

| Trustfulness | Distrustfulness |
| Scrupulousness | Unscrupulousness |
| Responsibility | Irresponsibility |

Now imagine these opposites in conflict!

Taking for granted that these people are *militant* in their beliefs and bound together by an unbreakable bond, what uproarious comedy or stark tragedy can be produced!

## Point of Attack

Some plays, novels, even short stories are so slow in starting that they seem as if they will never lead anywhere. We find ourselves so bored that we are ready to toss away the novel or leave the theater.

The point of attack should start your story. A story and especially a play must open with a crisis which is the sole point of attack—in the life or lives of one or more of the characters. A decision must be imminent and the characters must be ready to take action.

A married couple may quarrel bitterly for twenty years. They may threaten to leave each other. The question is: At what point in the lives of this couple would the author start his play? The answer is: When one of them is about to make a decision, or when the point of crisis is reached. Many things may have occurred between these people before we meet them. We are only interested in meeting them when they have reached a crisis in their lives and are about to take a decisive step.

Every short story, novel, and play should start in the middle of the middle. Read "The Killers" by Hemingway, or the play, *Born Yesterday*, by Garson Kanin. If you wish to write a good short story or novel, start on the note of crisis.

[ 19 ]

No law states that you cannot start your story in any other way. But if you want to catch the reader's interest *immediately*, you had better start with a conflict.

### Conflict

Even people who know little about the mechanics of writing are bored by a static play, a play which has little conflict or spotty conflict.

There are four types of conflict: foreshadowing, static, jumping, and slowly rising.

Foreshadowing conflict should appear at the beginning of the play. Crisis is the hint or the promise of future conflict. In the motion picture *Thirty Seconds Over Tokyo,* almost the entire picture consisted of foreshadowing conflict. The soldiers were training for a mission so dangerous that utmost secrecy was necessary. They weren't even allowed to discuss the mission among themselves. The soldiers' training, that could have been monotonous to watch, proved enrapturing to the audience because of the foreshadowing of the life or death mission planted in the very beginning.

In *Romeo and Juliet* the families were such bitter enemies that even the servants of the respective households were ready to kill each other on sight. What chance did the young lovers have?

When Nora in *A Doll's House* naïvely thought her husband Helmer would be grateful when she forged her father's signature to save his life, we waited for him to find out, knowing that Helmer was the epitome of honesty —and would never forgive.

Future events, future conflicts, must be foreshadowed at the beginning.

In static conflict the conflict remains on an even keel,

rising only momentarily. Since life constantly changes and nothing in life is ever static, static conflict is found only in bad writing.

Arguments and quarrels create static conflict, unless the characters are growing and changing during the arguments. Every movement, every line of dialogue must further the action toward the final goal.

In jumping conflict the characters jump from one emotional plane to another, eliminating the necessary transitional steps.

Nature never jumps. A seed planted in the soil one day does not produce a flower the next. During the interval many transitions take place before the plant finally blooms. In the play, the author plants the seeds of his characters' growth, and slowly step by step they grow, the changes being witnessed by the spectators.

Static and jumping are the two deadly mistakes of all writing. They must be avoided at all cost.

If you wish to avoid jumping or static conflict you must know in advance what road your characters must travel, for instance:

Drunkenness to sobriety
Sobriety to drunkenness
Timidity to brazenness
Brazenness to timidity
Simplicity to pretentiousness
Pretentiousness to simplicity
Fidelity to infidelity

The above represent two poles, the first the starting point, the second the arrival point. If you master this simple rule you'll have rising conflict throughout your story or play.

## Transition

Let us suppose that a character is going to travel from love to hate. Let us assume that there are nine emotional steps between the two poles of love and hate:

1. Love
2. Disappointment
3. Annoyance
4. Irritation
5. Disillusionment
6. Indifference
7. Disgust
8. Anger
9. Hate

If a character goes from No. 1 to No. 4, this constitutes jumping conflict. The author has neglected to show transitional steps Nos. 2 and 3. If the character then goes from No. 4 to No. 6, this is again jumping, because step No. 5 has been left out.

In real life a person may go through emotional changes in lightninglike fashion, so much so that his decision seems jumpy or hasty. This is not so. He has really gone through all the transitional steps, but so rapidly that it is not apparent. In fiction every step must be obvious and clearly shown.

When each character goes through each step, No. 1 to No. 10, then we have slowly rising conflict. Remember that each step must be higher than the succeeding one, just as each act gathers more momentum than the one before until the final curtain is reached.

## Crisis, Climax, Resolution

A play or story from beginning to end is a series of crises, climaxes, and resolutions. It begins with a crisis and builds up from there.

The crisis is a turning point, a time when a change is imminent. For example, in childbirth the birth pains are crisis, the birth is the climax, and the resolution is life or death.

Do you remember the play, *Rope's End,* by Patrick Hamilton? Two rich young men murder their schoolmate for the thrill and experience. As the curtain rises, they, the killers, are seen stuffing the murdered youth into a large chest. They invite the murdered youth's father in for a discussion in order to experience the thrill and danger that his visit will produce.

The play starts with a crisis as all plays and all good fiction writing should. A crisis is an unknown quantity, a turning point.

As the conflict in a play rises to meet each new crisis, climax and resolution, the author keeps building for the final crisis, climax and resolution, which will be the sum total of all the other crises, climaxes, and resolutions, proving the premise.

The first crisis is a minor one and proceeds to the second and third till it arrives at the greatest and final crisis.

If each succeeding crisis does not rise on an ascending scale, the conflict becomes static.

The final crisis, climax, and resolution can follow each other in rapid order at the end of the play or an interval can exist between them. In *A Doll's House* almost all of the third act constitutes resolution, as Nora explains to Helmer why she cannot remain. Even this resolution keeps transcending until the proud Helmer begs her forgiveness and begs Nora to stay. At this time a new crisis is created. Her refusal is the climax, and her departure the resolution.

The same principles apply to short stories and novels. While a short story consists of only one or two episodes, a novel may have hundreds, one after the other.

In a short story the tempo marches quickly, while in the novel it ambles along. But crisis, climax, and resolution are at work on the same general principle found in playwriting. Following are famous novelists and playwrights and their works for reference:

### Books

| | |
|---|---|
| *Bennett, Arnold* | The Old Wives' Tale |
| *Bowen, Elizabeth* | The Death of the Heart |
| *Cather, Willa* | My Antonia |
| | Death Comes for the Archbishop |
| | A Lost Lady |
| *Conrad, Joseph* | Nostromo |
| | The Nigger of the Narcissus |
| | Victory |
| *Dickens, Charles* | David Copperfield |
| *Dos Passos, John* | U.S.A. (The 42nd Parallel |
| | 1919 |
| | The Big Money) |
| *Dostoievsky* | The Brothers Karamazov |
| *Dreiser, Theodore* | An American Tragedy |
| | Sister Carrie |

## Books–continued

| | |
|---|---|
| *Faulkner, William* | The Wild Palms |
| | Intruder in the Dust |
| *France, Anatole* | Penguin Island |
| | Thaïs |
| | The Crime of Sylvestre Bonnard |
| *Fitzgerald, F. Scott* | The Great Gatsby |
| | Tender is the Night |
| *Forster, E. M.* | A Passage to India |
| *Galsworthy, John* | The Forsyte Saga |
| *Glasgow, Ellen* | Vein of Iron |
| *Gide, André* | The Counterfeiters |
| *Hemingway, Ernest* | A Farewell to Arms |
| | The Sun Also Rises |
| | For Whom the Bell Tolls |
| *Huxley, Aldous* | Point Counter Point |
| *James, Henry* | The Portrait of a Lady |
| | The Ambassadors |
| | Washington Square |
| *Joyce, James* | Ulysses |
| *Kipling, Rudyard* | Jungle Books |
| | Soldiers Three |
| | The Light That Failed |
| *Lewis, Sinclair* | Arrowsmith |
| | Main Street |
| | Babbitt |
| *London, Jack* | The Call of the Wild |

### Books—continued

| | |
|---|---|
| *Mann, Thomas* | Buddenbrooks |
| | The Magic Mountain |
| *Maugham, W. Somerset* | Of Human Bondage |
| *Melville, Herman* | Moby Dick |
| *Proust, Marcel* | Remembrance of Things Past |
| *Rolland, Romain* | Jean Christophe |
| *Tolstoi, Leo* | War and Peace |
| | Anna Karenina |
| *Twain, Mark* | Tom Sawyer |
| | Huckleberry Finn |
| *Undset, Sigrid* | Kristin Lavransdatter |
| *Wells, H. G.* | Tono-Bungay |
| *Wharton, Edith* | The Age of Innocence |
| | Ethan Frome |
| *Wilder, Thornton* | The Bridge of San Luis Rey |
| *Wolfe, Thomas* | Look Homeward, Angel |
| *Woolf, Virginia* | Mrs. Dalloway |
| *Zola, Émile* | Germinal |

### Plays

| | |
|---|---|
| *Barrie, Sir James M.* | What Every Woman Knows |
| *Barry, Philip* | The Philadelphia Story |
| *Boothe, Clare* | The Women |

### Plays—continued

| | |
|---|---|
| Chekhov, Anton | The Cherry Orchard |
| Connelly, Marc | The Green Pastures |
| | |
| Galsworthy, John | Loyalties |
| Green, Paul | In Abraham's Bosom |
| Gregory, Lady Augusta | The Rising of the Moon |
| | |
| Hauptmann, Gerhart | The Weavers |
| Hecht, Ben, and | |
| MacArthur, Charles | The Front Page |
| Hellman, Lillian | The Little Foxes |
| Housman, Laurence | Victoria Regina |
| Howard, Sidney | The Silver Cord |
| | Yellow Jack |
| | They Knew What They Wanted |
| | |
| Kaufman, George S. | The Royal Family |
| Kelly, George | Craig's Wife |
| Kesselring, Joseph | Arsenic and Old Lace |
| Kingsley, Sidney | Dead End |
| Kober, Arthur | Having Wonderful Time |
| | |
| Lindsay, Howard, and | |
| Crouse, Russel | Life With Father |
| | |
| Maeterlinck, Maurice | Pelléas and Mélisande |
| Maugham, W. Somerset | The Circle |
| | |
| Milne, A. A. | Mr. Pim Passes By |
| Odets, Clifford | Awake and Sing |
| | Golden Boy |
| | Waiting for Lefty |
| O'Neill, Eugene | Ah, Wilderness |

*Plays—continued*

| | |
|---|---|
| *Percy, Edward, and*<br>  *Denham, Reginald* | Ladies in Retirement |
| *Pinero, Sir Arthur Wing* | The Second Mrs. Tanqueray |
| *Sheriff, R. C.* | Journey's End |
| *Sherwood, Robert E.* | Abe Lincoln in Illinois<br>Idiot's Delight<br>The Petrified Forest |
| *Spewack, Bella and*<br>  *Samuel* | Boy Meets Girl |
| *Steinbeck, John* | Of Mice and Men |
| *Strindberg, August* | The Father |
| *Synge, John Millington* | Riders to the Sea |
| *Vane, Sutton* | Outward Bound |
| *Wilde, Oscar* | Lady Windermere's Fan |
| *Williams, Emlyn* | Night Must Fall<br>The Corn Is Green |
| *Williams, Tennessee* | The Glass Menagerie |

And the collected works of:

*George Bernard Shaw*

*Eugene O'Neill*

*John Galsworthy*

*Lillian Hellman*

# CHAPTER 4

# How to Eliminate Fear of Writing

SHE WAS well read, intelligent; her imagination functioned smoothly and efficiently; she was honest and had what was of prime importance to a writer, humility. Still, everything she wrote came out stilted and unnatural.

What was wrong? Fear? Fear of failure?

Fear is the natural enemy of man. The insecurity of our existence, the ever-changing environment, keeps us constantly on our toes. Fear of failure is an ever-present companion of not only the student writer but the professional writer as well. Fear creates tenseness and mental constipation in writers. How can you do away with this curse, this legitimate child of fear?

She need only to say to herself with determination, "I am writing for my own amusement and if it turns out badly, none will be the wiser. I may tear it up if I wish, or hide it from hostile eyes, and that will be the end of it."

But despite giving herself this good advice, the young woman could not think of herself as anything but a failure.

She could not shake off the fear of ridicule. She had a good reason for it, too. She had told her friends that she had signed up at a school for a course in writing. What would they say, if she were a failure? She tried and tried to make good, but she became worse instead. All her efforts were in vain.

I knew that I had to do something to restore her confidence in herself. I told her to write down any conversation she would have with anyone, on any day of the week.

"Won't it be a waste of time?" she asked. "After all, recording a conversation is only a simple, mechanical task which can be done by anyone."

I assured her that it was not so, because whatever recording she made would filter through her mind first and then reflect her own observational power, her intelligence, her selectivity, and her taste.

She was skeptical, but she followed my advice. Her first attempt was a little gem.

For the first time, she was free from the fear of ridicule. She had given her talent a chance to function without fear. Here's the little piece: See for yourself if it is not good writing. The character she portrays speaks as this particular character should. There's nothing stilted about this writing.

### The Maid

There was a knock at the door and I opened it to admit the maid. The middle-aged woman walked in carrying her broom and pail.

"Good morning," she said as she put her broom down.

"Good morning," I answered. "How do you feel today?" I asked, since she had been suffering with a cold the week before.

"Oh, I feel better but it's not all cleared up yet. The doctor gave me a shot of pen'cillun," she rubbed her buttocks hard and explained further. "These days anything happens the doctor gives you a shot of pen'cillun and it takes care of it."

I tried to get dressed but her conversation again demanded my attention.

"Everyone has the flu these days. Even young people . . . and you know even if you get a shot of pen'cillun you have to stay in for twenty-four hours or it doesn't do any good."

She seemed very impressed with the word "penicillin" even if she did have a hard time pronouncing it. It seemed she was very excited that such a wonderful drug discovery was found in her lifetime.

"Well, you should stay home for a few days and get over it," I said as I adjusted one stocking on my leg.

She looked straight at me through her thick glasses and spoke with a little antagonism.

"The housekeeper here doesn't believe you that you're sick unless you're dying. She thinks because nothing ever happens to her that no one else ever gets sick."

She took a step forward to emphasize the importance of what she had to say.

"Y'know last year I got run over and they took nine stitches in my head." She pointed to her head and then submitted it to me to feel and took my hand in hers to find the right spot.

"Feel it?" she asked.

I nodded and she went on.

"Well, when they took me to the emergency hospital and said I'd have to be out for a week, she was real mad." A small smile came over her face as she adjusted a bobby pin in her grey hair, and stood up a little straighter. "But then a few months later she got run over . . . getting off the bus at 57th and Lexington. Her leg was hurt. She had to stay in the hospital for two weeks. . . . Y'know with a leg it takes a long time. But even on crutches she came to work. Some people just can't stay in. Well, anyway, then she knew what it was like."

I looked at her and saw a woman who in her earlier days might have been quite nice looking but the years of hard work had worn her down. She wasn't finished telling me of how fate gets even with those who have no sympathy for others so she continued.

"Y'know, twelve years ago I went to the dentist. Oh— I had such trouble. My head hurt—y'know when your teeth bother you your head hurts," she explained, almost proud of her knowledge. "The dentist said I'd have to pull my teeth—not one at a time but two and three. He said I had py'rea and they were all so little, they'd have to be pulled. So I started. One day when I was in such pain, I came home. And y'know, my husband who should have said, 'you stay in bed and I'll bring you hot water or cold water or whatever you want'—well, y'know what he said to me when I was suffering so?" She didn't wait for me to ask but went right on. "He said, 'you stink and you smell.' That was what he said. So now he's having his teeth pulled and he goes around holding his mouth.

"When he complains I just tell him that he stinks and he smells like he told me. You cannot receive sympathy when you don't give any, I told him. So he doesn't say anything—just holds his mouth. Now he knows what it feels like." She shook her head and picked up the pail and walked towards the bathroom.

As I watched her leaning over the bathtub and scrubbing away I thought of the little apartment she lived in, and her husband came into focus—a man in his late fifties probably—and walking around the house with his suspenders hanging from his trousers and holding his hand to his jaw in silent pain.

Since writing this little story she has written many more character sketches, each one better than the last. She has managed to shake off at last the paralyzing fear of failure and ridicule.

Bertrand Russell said: "To conquer fear is the begining of wisdom." Perhaps. But one thing I know to be sure: If you conquer fear, at least you give yourself a fighting chance to become a better writer.

Now, the question is, what kind of exercises does a writer need? Where does he look for them?

You don't have to go on any treasure hunt. Just write verbatim every day the conversations you have had, or what you have overheard during the day. Forget all rules and regulations while you are making these notes. Jot them down in any way, even if they turn out to be repetitious.

Then try to recapture the person you are writing about, so the reader can actually see him. Tell something about the clothing he wore and its condition. Was the person to whom you were speaking an excited, or a cold, detached, or a humorous person? In what mental state did you find him?

How did you meet him? Did you meet him accidentally on the avenue? Was it a business or a residential section? What day of the week? Was the person complaining that no one understood him, or was he boasting about how great he was? You might as well know that whatever this person said, there was a purpose behind it. He either wanted your admiration or your sympathy.

Try to recapture that person in his entirety. Even if nothing dramatic occurred at the time of your conversation, the story will still be good reading.

It is a rare privilege for anyone to look behind the masks we all wear and to see man's motivations. If you've done this, you have accomplished a rare thing. You've drawn a physical and mental picture of a living, pulsating human being. This is the hardest thing to accomplish and the most envied form of writing in the profession.

While you do this daily exercise, you cannot help but accumulate inestimable information for future use. If you have a discussion with a nurse, she will no doubt use medical expressions common to her profession. If you mark down these expressions you will be richer with the knowledge of something you did not know before. You should follow the same procedure with lawyers, truck drivers, janitors, etc. Follow this same procedure at home, with your mother, etc. Their usage of words, their remarks, are those of authentic, genuine people. Their outlook on life will greatly help you.

Now, to answer the question, over what period of time one should note down conversations? Great writers never stop. G. B. Shaw, Hawthorne, Ibsen, Chekhov, and other well-known writers, past or present, always had fat notebooks filled with character sketches and other kinds of writings.

This daily diary will become a good source of information for a writer to use throughout his lifetime. This routine of writing daily will help you to formulate with great ease and freedom of expression whatever you want to say.

[ 34 ]

Now let me tell you about another talented student. Writing came easy to him. All his writings consisted of lurid tales about the South Seas, Spain, and France. They concerned Negroes, Communists, and many subjects about which he knew nothing.

He had style, imagination, and wrote with great dexterity, but still his stories were flat. He could never create a living human being.

After awhile, I convinced him it would be wiser if he wrote about some prosaic character he knew. He did! Finally he learned that good writing, even success, does not lie in writing about Spain or sun-baked Africa, which he knows nothing about, but in character portrayal and in people he knows quite intimately.

Here is his first attempt.

### Carl Frank

I sat down for coffee and a cigarette at a table with four or five men. Joe was talking business with a couple of Production Department men, but he didn't have much interest because he was going back in the Navy soon.

Carl Frank came and sat down opposite me. He listened absently to Joe's talk for a minute, then he leaned forward to speak confidently to me. "Joe isn't really interested," he said. "After July 6th it'll take a five cent stamp to catch up to him if they want to tell him their troubles."

At the mention of his name Joe turned to Carl Frank. "Huh?"

Carl grinned at me. "He don't get it," he said. Joe turned back to the Production Department men and Carl was silent.

"Carl," I asked, "you must be out in the open air a

[ 35 ]

lot, no? Your color—you're pretty well tanned all the time."

Carl is a stocky man of about fifty with light blue eyes in a browned and wrinkled face.

"Oh, sure," he said. He took a pipe and a can of tobacco from the high pocket of his khaki colored pants and began to fill it and light up. Carl's uniform as foreman of the Chocolate Coating Department, is khaki pants and shirt, no distinguishing marks or emblems, but as a supervisor he is not required to wear the standard factory cap. His shirt was open at the collar exposing a neck and chest equally tanned. "Flowers," Carl explained. "I got a lot of flowers."

"Guess they keep you busy," I suggested.

Carl was puffing at his pipe then and he slouched down in his chair more comfortably.

"Lot of work," Carl went on. "I'm out there every night —week ends—three or four hours every night." There was a gleam, a sort of amused superior look, in Carl's eyes that told me that Carl could relate some pretty interesting and amazing facts about flowers if he wanted to start. He seemed to be turning over in his mind the question of whether I was a potential worthwhile audience or just making casual, polite and disinterested remarks. He puffed in silence, his brown hands quiet on the table before him.

Carl's hair, rather sparse and bleached to an uneven light brown by the sun, was too thin and dry to lie flat on his head. His face was expressive, mobile, with a rather loose mouth and full lips. There was a deep cleft in the chin and a hint of dimples in his cheeks, though the face was wrinkled and seamed to a point where dimples became long grooves between the nose and mouth.

I prodded Carl gently with another question. "You must

have a lot of ground to work on. Don't you get tired after working here all day?"

"No!" Carl exploded. "I like it!" He removed the pipe from his mouth and sat forward. "I got a schedule. Now, take last week—I was transplanting. I got two rows of larkspur." Here Carl looked off toward the end of the room and gestured with his pipe. "Rows as long as from the wall to this table—took me a heck of a time—I got out there with a sprinkler." Carl was off on his best subject and I let him run awhile.

As he talked I watched him, his face mostly. Carl has always been remote from most of us. He's a man who does his work quietly and goes about his own business without mixing very much with other men. I had heard some time ago that Carl Frank had a bad heart, was a little strange in his attitude toward others who worked with him, and also, recently, that his wife had died. The few times I had occasion to talk to him, mostly on business, he had seemed to bear out the general view as to his strange attitude. I would say he was a man of little formal education, long experience in chocolate coatings but really no technical knowledge that could be traced to any book of scientific research, and firmly grounded opinions in all matters.

I wondered if Carl missed his wife—if he thought of her when he was working on his flowers. As he talked, he was absorbed in what he was telling me—rather he was absorbed in telling, for his expressions showed that he was sharing with me some of his cleverness, his persistence, his knack in raising flowers. "I watched them Holland planters—I see how they do it. They're out in the rain transplanting. They wear slickers and boots. Water comin' down all around and they keep plantin'!"

He snapped his big fingers. "You ought to see how them flowers shoot up. That's how they do it. I transplanted larkspur last week. Thousands of 'em. So small—" he hunted in his shirt pocket unsuccessfully, then held up a rigid little finger—"like a pencil. They're even hard to see, they're so small." He bent over, putting his nose almost to the table.

"You got to get down close. I used a big sprinkler and put plenty of water down when I transplant." Carl now held up a thick forefinger and then turned his hand over as though poking a hole in the topsoil. "Not one of 'em even drooped!"

I could see Carl had opened the floodgates. His eyes were dancing—he neglected his pipe. He tapped on the table to emphasize a point, snapped his fingers to show how quickly a tricky bit of gardening succeeded, stretched a big arm out to show how vast was his empire or how evenly a bed of flowers grew. He was far away from chocolate coatings. I rather imagined he was far away from his wife and his bad heart.

I had to get back to my desk. I dropped my cigarette in my saucer and rose. "Got to get back," I said.

Carl put his pipe back in his mouth and puffed. His eyes were still again, his face quietly composed. I think he was far away from me, too.

This writer stopped writing about far-off countries and about people he knew little, and came back into the fold instead. He had learned a lesson he'd never forget.

The class applauded heartily when he finished his reading, and notwithstanding some slight criticism, the class in general agreed that he had written a fine character study.

[ 38 ]

Since then, he too has written more brilliant stories than the above, but I have intentionally chosen this very first attempt to point out what an unbelievable difference it makes, if a person writes about a subject with which he is familiar, even in his first attempt.

After all, people not only represent reality, but are the subject about which one knows. Even in allegory, farce, or fantasy, a writer needs characters that the readers can recognize as familiar or real.

The writer of "Carl Frank" escaped into a fantasy, because he felt he could never describe real people or conquer reality. Now he knows it is much easier to write about people he knows and more fun, too, than those lurid tales about nonexistent one-dimensional characters he formerly wrote about.

There isn't any law against writing weird stories or plays if they're based on facts about real people with human traits and human impulses.

Try to remain on familiar ground with your writing and—don't advertise the fact that you want to be a writer. Your fears will slowly die from neglect.

CHAPTER 5

# *How to Select*
# *Your Subject*

Intimate knowledge of an event carries in itself the universality of identification with ourselves.

Read the classics, and you'll find that the characters we remember most are the ones we know the best. A character, a universal character, that is, is one whom we known as intimately as is humanly possible. The differences between a Greek, a Spaniard, a Hungarian, and an Englishman are their national customs or traditions. Beyond that they are all human like everyone else on this globe.

To know what lifts a character or a trivial affair into becoming a poignant, living human experience will help us greatly toward writing a good, significant play or story.

The question, now, is how to go about selecting the right subject about which to write.

A famous writer would know what he wants to write about. He is at all times sure of his likes and dislikes. A great writer is always on the warpath against the world. He constantly tries to prove something. The world might think he is wrong, but the great writer thinks otherwise, and his conviction is enough of an impetus for him to start to prove it.

No writer can be indifferent toward his own subject. He must believe in his project's feasibility. He must prove this in his writing. A writer must be biased, otherwise his reasoning will carry no conviction. All great crusaders were and will be biased.

A writer needs a blind, uncompromising faith in his own work. If a writer's conviction is dependent upon the opinion of another person, then he is a hopelessly weak character. He is not made of the granitelike material of which a writer needs to be fashioned.

Knowledge will give you the courage to withstand the misguided efforts of well-meaning people who are dying to "help" you out of your "difficulties."

Whatever you wish to write, in any form, should be from your own conviction. I would like to repeat this simple fact over and over again. Conviction is the real foundation of all creation.

The subject you want to write about, then, must be one of your own rock-bottom convictions. It is so easy to write about something you know so well that it actually haunts you.

Do you have a theme like that? Do you love or hate one thing more than anything else? Do you feel that there are injustices in this world? Would you like to see man or society improved? Do you find people too materialistic or too idealistic? Are you for or against any of this?

Whatever your conviction, if it is a conviction, it is the right one for you. To hate or to love something or

[ 41 ]

someone is a slow-growing process. One, two, three, and many, many more facts may pile up before their sheer weight influences you to do something about them.

A conviction is not necessarily a universal truth; far from it. A conviction might be as unpopular as a disease, but if you believe in it and are willing to fight for it, you may change or influence others who will then be willing to aid in the fight for your cause.

Yes, my friend, you have guessed it—a conviction means propagandizing something in which the author believes. All great works of art are forms of propaganda. These forms of propaganda are for the betterment of mankind and are never antisocial.

Believe it or not, there was a time when the teaching of elementary writing in schools caused bloody riots. To teach the most elementary scientific facts was also forbidden. Women's fight for equality with man was a most heated, controversial topic for decades . . . it still is. Lives were sacrificed in the struggle to liberate the slaves. To fight against greediness, tyranny, or any of the human excesses is as necessary today as it was in the past.

Even if a writer isn't aiming to write the best novel or the best play in the history of writing, one thing is certain: he wants to write a good one. He must first remember, then, that above all he must know his character more thoroughly, even, than he knows himself. Secondly, the writer must know that nothing ever happens without good sound motivation. Thirdly, whatever a writer writes, it must be of his own conviction. A conviction is the backbone of all writing.

You have chosen your subject. It is something you believe in 100 per cent. But you still don't know how to start your story.

I wonder how many writers know that every story must have a foundation, the same as a house must have one. The foundation in any form of story is the character or characters who carry the author's conviction.

Since the purpose of this chapter is to show how to approach and unfold a story or a play, I might as well give you an example about how to draw a character. A moment ago I said that a character is the foundation of your story, so you should know how strong this foundation has to be, and how much necessary information you must have about this person who is going to be not merely the foundation of the story but the story itself.

Any character you choose will live his own individual life. But strangely enough, he wants and will fight until death if necessary for the very things the author himself wants and will fight for. In short, this character is really your *alter ego*. He is you! Remember, you can't write about things you don't know. Through your imagination, you are going to live the life of your character, and in return your character will represent no one else but you, in reality.

An evil character, whom you abhor and wish to destroy, nonetheless will represent your conception of evil, and since your conception is part of your thought process—crystallized through your experiences, part of you—he will represent you and your conception of evil.

We might as well understand each other as much as possible. Every character you write about will represent your conception of yourself and the world. If you are inexperienced, naïve, or ignorant of facts pertaining to your character, it will be evident that it is you, not your characters, who is naïve or stupid.

Let me put it in a different way: every character you

write about will be a reflection, like that you see in a mirror, of your own innermost self.

If a writer agrees with me on this score, it means that he has made up his mind not to write about anything of which he hasn't thorough knowledge.

# CHAPTER 6

# *Characters*

In a previous chapter I dealt with three-dimensional characters. Now I wish to discuss the difference between character and characteristics.

Many people have no conception of who or what a "character" is. Must a human being be peculiar, eccentric, or crazy for us to stamp him a "character"? Not necessarily. If you happen to be fastidious or sloppy and another person deems to call you "peculiar," you become a "character" to him—but not necessarily to everybody else.

Now, what is the difference between a "character" and a "characteristic"? None whatsoever, because the outstanding characteristic of a man makes him a character. A big nose is as characteristic, for instance, as honesty.

Every living human being possesses some kind of characteristics that eventually stamp him for some people as being "different," in short, a "character." Deformities or perfections, for that matter, are equally characteristic.

A writer must look further to discover mannerisms too. Peculiar qualities are a great help in characterizing people. Any kind of idiosyncrasy makes a man a distinct character.

Although every human being represents all the good and bad qualities inherited from his ancestors, there *must be* one outstanding quality, good or bad, that will stamp him for what he really is. This singular characteristic will necessarily overshadow all other inherent characteristics, and must stand out like a sore thumb for everyone to see, except, of course, the person himself.

Here are a few examples of people with characteristic behaviorisms. I am purposely leaving out the man with the ever-present pimples on his face, or those who dress peculiarly, or those who are physically different. I am concentrating solely on the mentally eccentric, obviously "individualistic characters."

The man who is proud that he is never excited. (This is obviously an impossibility, but that's what he claims.)

The man who never forgets a single word that is spoken to him. (No doubt a terrific exaggeration.)

The man who hates convention.

The man who thinks that the majority of mankind is stupid.

The man who hates children.

The man who thinks he can do everything better than anyone else.

The man who wants to become primitive.

The man who believes in spiritualism, and hates all materialists.

The man who believes in materialism and fights against spiritualism.

The woman who cannot say "no."

The woman who feels that men are inferior to women.

The woman who hates her own sex.

The woman who despises housewives.

The woman who considers marriage a legal prostitution.

[ 46 ]

A housewife who demands double pay for overtime work, be it manual or sexual.

The man who can judge people by their faces.

The dignified man who loses control the moment he sees a pretty face.

The man who is hurt if you fail to laugh at his insipid jokes.

The man who tries to make friends by obvious flattery.

The man who tells the wrong thing at the wrong time to the right person.

The man who thinks women are good only for one purpose.

The man who falls all over himself to please.

The man who thinks that milk is poison to grownups, and warns everyone who's willing to listen.

The man who believes that the great majority of people are honest only because they're afraid to break the law.

The man who thinks he was born to do bigger things than what he is doing now.

The woman who thinks that she's eternally misunderstood.

The woman who would wither away without gossip.

The man who believes in reincarnation.

All these people are characters. Why do they behave like this? For a very good reason. They wish to arouse interest in themselves.

We all, without exception, wish to be important. But all this will be discussed fully in motivation. Let it suffice to say now that the above characters are the ones who make themselves felt wherever they are. They're the aggressive types.

But there are other types too. The shy ones, the recluses, and the abusive ones. And there are the eternally excited, the religious fanatics, and the comedians who would do anything for a laugh. I am sure you know the smiling and silly-looking optimist, and the sneering pessimist, and the hordes of other kinds of people known as "characters."

The strangest thing is that, if you care to look, you're liable to discover a little bit of all this madness in yourself too.

When you and I and the rest of the crowd decide that someone else

    is a clown;

    is crooked;

    is a failure;

    is a show-off;

    is a success;

    is a philanderer;

    is a liar;

    is honest;

    is a genius;

then the so-and-so pulls a very surprising and very neat trick out of the bag:

    The clown turns out to be a real thinker.

    The crook reforms and gives himself up.

    The failure becomes a huge success.

    The show-off turns out to be a very modest man.

    The success turns out to be a total failure.

    The philanderer was really loyal.

    The liar wished to cover up his friend's mistake.

    The honest one was really crooked.

    The genius was just a flash in the pan.

This example shows, I hope, clearly enough that no one is for twenty-four hours

    a clown

    crooked

a failure
a show-off
a success
a philanderer
a liar
honest
a genius.

## II

I was discussing the general bone structure of a character in class when a bright young member of the group exclaimed, "Mr. Egri, would you mind being more explicit about this subject."

Everyone in the class agreed that character building was one of the hardest things to understand and execute.

"Speaking for myself," she continued, "I've been sweating it out for days on a character outline and still when I bring it into class the verdict invariably is: not three-dimensional, which means in our lingo that it is not a living character. Am I right so far, Mr. Egri?" she asked.

"Yes," I replied, "you are. But what is it explicitly you want explained? I have illustrated to all of you the basic principles of character over and over again. However, you must now experiment, write and write until it hurts, and continue reading the books I have suggested to you."

"All right then," said the young lady, who is a promising newspaper reporter. "Something must be wrong with me because I . . ."

"It's not always so," I answered. "My experience has been that many people, even the most talented, have difficulty with character drawing. Why is it so hard?" I asked this rhetorical question myself and answered it. "It is so difficult," I continued, "because the writer's business is not only to create a lifelike human being, but to make him coexist with other people in his natural habitat. That is not as simple as it sounds.

"A man might act well-behaved and tolerant in public, but behave belligerently in his home life. In every human life the contradiction is the norm. When you observe a man shouting and abusing people in his office, would you guess that he is a charming and a gracious man at home? Hardly! But yet, it is possible.

"A human being—any human being," I continued, "is complex, contradictory. No man is easy to catch in his totality. Let me give you an example," I said, as I stood up in front of the class. "Many of my students told me time and time again that they never saw anyone with such patience as I have." I paused for a split second and smiled. "But it will surprise you to know," I continued, "when I tell you that it is poppycock—I am a very impatient man, indeed."

The class gaped at me, stunned. "I am short-tempered," I continued, "and this is only one of my great faults!"

There was a prolonged silence. "What you should never forget is that no living person is an angel or a devil," I repeated; "that every one of us is capable of committing the most horrible deed, if we find ourselves in a dangerous situation, and only by committing this deed can we save ourselves.

"That being the case, I wonder how many different kinds of people lie dormant in us.

"Let us try an experiment," I said. "I want you to write on a piece of paper some shortcomings of some people you know."

John S. interrupted almost instantly with, "Why not write our own shortcomings? We know them best."

"That is what I really wanted you to do, but I was afraid that the request might have embarrassed you," I answered.

"Not at all," came the answer in unison.

"All right then, make a list of all your shortcomings, or at least as many as you can think of now. I'll leave the room while you are doing it. Don't sign your names to the paper, and when they are finished mix them up and place them on my desk."

I gave them identical sheets of yellow paper and left the room. Fifteen minutes later when I returned I still found them writing. I guessed that they must have a great many shortcomings. I had to stop them for lack of time. To my surprise, they all signed their names, without exception, to what I almost called their confessionals . . . because that's what they really were.

As I hurriedly glanced through a few of the papers I was struck by the sheer honesty of their contents. It made me feel good. It meant that they were not only honest and sincere with themselves, but that they shared closeness and rare intimacy with me and with each other. They had confessed their shortcomings, which is usually something we all try to disguise with many subterfuges.

I guessed what had happened! No doubt, in their zeal to at least understand character, they were ready to dig down even into their own vitals, as a form of punishment, tinged with masochism too, for their many failures. It now appeared as if they were ready to go to any limit to find out what character is composed of.

They asked me to read the papers on which their names

appeared. I did, and I'll quote a few of the shortcomings they listed.

The first paper was written by a competent and energetic young woman, always solid as a rock and always composed. She wrote something about herself which we would have never dreamed. Her paper listed: lazy, nervous, hypersensitive, lying to cover up deficiencies, self-contempt, nervousness again, no guts, procrastination, sadistic pleasure in burning up a few selective people, bad loser, etc.

There was a beginning of a new sentence, which she hadn't had time to finish because I had called a halt. Now everyone turned to her. She looked defiantly into the eyes of the members of the class. There wasn't any sign of shame or regret written on her face. She seemed rather proud and relieved that she had had the guts to say aloud, at last, what she had always been afraid to even mention to herself.

"Self-contempt, no guts," my own voice re-echoed her words. I had never seen a more self-assured woman, a more forward-thinking and -acting person than she was. There were a barrelful of contradictions in that young lady's assertions of her shortcomings.

I started to read the next paper. This one was by a charming young man of about thirty-five. He was dependable, straightforward, honest, and very lovable. Here is what he had to say: "Lazy," I started to read, but stopped instinctively, and almost immediately, before I could utter another word, a thought flashed through my mind. "Funny, very funny. Why in the world does he say he's lazy, when, as far as I know, he isn't. He appears to be the most industrious student in the entire class."

I began to read his paper again. "Lazy, procrastinator,

egotist, vain, possessive, liar, superficial, self-love, self-pity . . ."

I stopped reading and looked at the author of this self-confession. No, apparently there wasn't any trace of the person he said he was, in his appearance at least.

The confessions as I read them one after the other sounded as if they had been written by one person. The old theory that all of us were more or less alike, the difference being only in degree, seemed to really be true.

Now, I wish you, too, would ask yourself: "Do I have all those traits listed by the students as their own?" Did you ever hate, love, feel jealous or greedy? If you did, you belong in the same class. Anyhow, list all the shortcomings you think you possess. Then, and then only, will you agree with me that you, too, are the same, to some degree, as other human beings.

But let me illustrate further. Here is another young man, a playwright, of about thirty-five. He made a notation under his own name, "All mine," and listed the following!

"Laziness, procrastination, impatience with the failure on the part of others to see my point. Basically, a part of my own unwillingness to admit that I am wrong or have not explained myself properly. Failure to put first things first, that is, I am too easily diverted by unimportant details. Willingness to be satisfied with something less than the best I can do. Tendency to vent feeling of self-annoyance on innocent bystanders. Selfishness, irresponsibility, lack of assurance about writing."

It was at this point that he, too, had stopped writing, to comply with my request. Now, the interesting part is that almost all felt that they were "lazy" and champion "procrastinators." Why this recurring self-accusation of laziness by the entire class? Apparently these writers felt that although they wrote a great deal (and I am a witness to the fact that they really did), they knew more than anyone else that they could have done much better had they only applied themselves more.

The incentive in their cases, then, is a clear-cut goal or premise for their lives. They want to be writers and playwrights of the first caliber. *Ergo,* they must work harder and longer than others who have not set such a high goal for themselves.

I am practically sure that everyone feels the same way about himself when a projected work is not accomplished in record time. Obviously this is a sign of guilt.

All human beings are a mixture of good and bad. Goodness in human beings, as a pure and unalloyed trait, is nonexistent. Badness, or just being bad, is impossible. Someone might protest that he is completely angelic. Let him protest. It will prove that this person hasn't any conception of even the most elementary form of psychology. Nothing in nature appears in its pure form. Why should man then be the only exception?

It is of the utmost importance to prove to a writer that everyone in existence is more or less the same, even if he comes from a different nationality or from a wildly divergent atmospheric locality. Human beings remain human beings in any part of the world. A writer should not be afraid to approach any other human being because he feels alien toward him. Behind his strange customs, traditions, or laws is a human being, the same human being to be found anywhere on the globe.

If a writer finds it hard to draw a three-dimensional character, it is because he forgets that the character in question is really himself, in a different setting, under a different name.

# CHAPTER 7

# Observation

THE POWER of observation is an indispensable tool for a writer, and curiosity is the mother of observation. Curiosity is a sign of an inner hunger which can never be completely satisfied.

Are you interested in watching a painter paint his picture? Of course you are. I hope you have seen one struggle through days, weeks, even months to evolve one satisfactory color combination. A real artist tries very, very hard to give us his best.

Through the eyes of a painter, we common mortals discover a new and exciting world—the enchanting world of colors. A painter—and artist—teaches us what to look for in nature and how to enjoy ourselves better.

You must always be observing and always be curious if you want to be a good writer.

And there are musicians and composers—who teach us how to discover harmony in chaos and chaos in harmony. The musicians are really the ears of mankind. They translate all the magic sounds into something tangible—something we wouldn't have noticed or otherwise enjoyed.

Are you curious now to know what a writer teaches mankind? A writer teaches all that a musician and painter do—and more. He shows people, themselves, as they are, or as other people see them. The writer makes people see, hear, feel and recapture what was good or bad, vital or beautiful, in their lives.

Remember to be curious!

It's of great interest, for instance, to observe how persons in the street walk. No two people ever walk in the same way. As in everything else, the varieties of walking are endless. To walk is to move. The body draws a line in space. It creates a rhythm, and every move tells its own story. Every movement is really music. If you observe carefully, a simple movement will tell you about the person in question. The movement may be a frivolous one, a sagging one, or a joyful one.

Watch people talk. It is fascinating to watch the gestures of their hands or the tilting of their heads, as they blend into a symphony.

Do you notice people's clothing? You should. It tells you volumnes about its wearer.

When you go into a strange home, you can know about the person living there before you have been introduced to him, even before you have seen him.

Surroundings are the mirrors of the inhabitants.

*Observe! Observe!*

Even in the home of poverty-stricken people there must be a sign of or at least a weak attempt at beauty, if the occupants have any feeling for beauty in them . . . an attempt toward improvement, revealing the real nature of the people living there.

No, people cannot hide their true identity. In fact, they

never try to hide it. Whenever they leave their homes, no matter how neatly clothed, they are still an open book.

The difference between a moron and a very talented man is that, whereas one doesn't even see the obvious, the other can penetrate the deepest recesses of your mind and heart.

But first you must be curious.

Voices tell their own story. There are a million different kinds of voices. You may never think of it this way, but it is true, nevertheless, that voices are only containers for words, as red blood corpuscles are carriers for oxygen.

Some voices are framed by robust muscles; they boom like trumpets, carry their messages with graceful ease. You do not see voices, but you know them as well as if you had seen them. Some are pale and wrinkled; some just stumble along, leaning on crutches, as if they were on the verge of dying. And there are voices which sound like dizzy ballet dancers in the air; they pirouette; they out-leap Nijinsky. And there are voices that have a touch of magic, transferring sound into a velvety caress. These voices embrace you and soothe you.

There are fat, ugly, growling voices; there are laughing, sighing, shivering, crying voices; there are bragging and wailing voices. Voices are vulnerable as they linger or hurry their precious cargo through the air.

There are a million exciting little trivialities all around you. They become important, though, when you start to build and characterize and dramatize the characters in your story or play. A missing button on a man's overcoat might indicate the solution of a murder mystery or simply imply a sloppy and indifferent person.

Are you interested in flowers, birds, trees? You should be. They are all around you and are a part of your life.

Your character might not give a hoot for all the birds in the world, but his very annoyance by them will help you to establish a character trait peculiar to that man.

Be curious! Always be curious!

Find out why some people wear loud colors—why others stick to gray and dark, moody materials. There is more than one reason for this.

A writer must be a detective first.

Find the clues to the personalities of your characters. For instance, why one feels abused; why another can't walk a step without being dignified; why one is abusive or conceited; why one always insists that he's in the right; or why one always insists upon being a perfectionist; etc.

You should be curious enough to discover why persons act like they do and then you will discover the secret of great writing.

# CHAPTER 8

# *Motivation—I*

A MAN, a carpenter, let us say, killed his wife and his two young children and then committed suicide. This *two-line news item* in the papers can be enlarged to four, even ten, pages of colorful and hair-raising reporting and still the reader hasn't the slightest idea why that terrible carnage had to happen.

Let me imagine what could have been the immediate reason for this desperate act. I emphasize "immediate," because there are more reasons under the surface. The man might have been incurably sick, with a morbid fear that his family would become dependent on public charity as his own family had been in his early childhood. They would be better off dead, he decided, than to live in such dire misery. (The motivation seems sound from his sick point of view.)

Religious fanaticism could have been another reason. He might have been obsessed with the sin of man. Life is hard and cruel and makes men crawl, lie, cheat, be carnal, and at the end blaspheme the good Lord and kill just to remain alive. He can't bear the thought that his innocent children should be forced into such horrible sins. He wants them to go to heaven instead of hell and kills them while he can be sure of their absolute salvation. (This too can be accepted as a sound but sick motivation for a sick mind.)

There is still another possible reason. The man might kill because he loves another woman, wants to be free, but remorse overcomes him and he kills himself too. (We can see such motivations every day.)

He is jealous. His wife wants to leave him and life becomes meaningless, so he kills. (This is the most frequent motivation.)

Every flower has its root in the soil. We see the flowers and we name them: jealousy, greed, hate, etc.; but writers usually forget the root, the origin of conflict, as it reaches down into the earth to feed the flower.

All the reasons I have mentioned above are only the flowers, not the roots. The writer has to find, if not all, at least most of the reasons why and how this emotion could have grown so big.

Love, hate, greed, and all other emotions are only the visible by-products of deep inner conflicts. Let me examine "jealousy," to pick one out of many violent manifestations of disturbed emotions, and ask: why did this have to happen, why should this man be jealous? How did it start, and when? Jealousy, like everything else, requires time to grow. Transition in emotion, as in nature, never jumps, but takes its time to become relentless hatred or jealousy that kills.

If you're looking for reasons, just think of *everyday* neglect, cruelty, discrimination, hunger, humiliation, and many such unpleasant *common* experiences. They are the hotbeds of hatred and violence. But all this usually starts in early childhood and leaves an indelible scar as one grows older, like a tattoo mark on a child that expands as he grows.

One might miss all these ugly manifestations of life and still be infected with a haunting fear and humility. How come?

One might have big nose, hands, or feet. And this will be enough for one to feel the burning, the gnawing resentment of those who were disinherited from the family of man.

One might be bald, or have a slight murmur in his heart, or he might be too short or too tall, or have any one of thousands of very childish, little, inconsequential imperfections which would merit a smile if spoken of, but become a tragedy when one broods over them.

A writer might justifiably ask: Is there any man or woman who would be completely satisfied with himself? No, there is no such animal. So most of us are in a perpetual wonder, and we consider it a miracle if anyone is so shortsighted as to fall in love with us. Naturally we live in a constant fear, and dread the time when our beloved is going to fed up with such a miserable creature as we happen to be.

There are degrees of fear, of course. Now, let me find out a few facts about this particular jealous man, who killed. What was his ideal woman, for instance? What kind of a woman did he admire in his youth? Was he looking for his mother, his sister, some actress, or—it sounds ridiculous but it happens—is he looking for the image of some famous murderess?

If you read newspaper accounts you must know that the man who kills a couple of women receives many letters from women, offering themselves in marriage. Men make the same propositions to murderesses.

Now, whether we know it or not, we all have preconceived ideas of beauty, dignity, style, elegance, friendship, and loyalty. And sometimes we go through life looking for just such a particular ideal.

People usually admire something they *missed* in their lives. So the woman the jealous man killed might have had something peculiar about her that tremendously excited him at the beginning of their courtship. You might think it strange if I say that a man might fall in love with a woman who walks, or talks, or laughs in a certain way. The color scheme of a woman's dress, or love of sport, music, or dancing can be the starting point of a romance.

Of course such trivial attraction, even if it is coupled with sex appeal, cannot and should not be the foundation for a permanent relationship. But the majority of people still marry on such flimsy motivation.

The jealous man who killed his wife no doubt was trying to escape from imaginary or real danger, or a felony, perhaps, or from a life he hated—when he first ran into the arms of this woman. Whatever the motivation was, he in his shortsightedness or outright ignorance must have thought that with this marriage he achieved at last comparative safety for himself. That safety might have meant financial stability, mental equilibrium, or both.

But when he realized, in a frenzy of fear, that instead of "safety" he had run into a "trap," which was fed by intermittent quarreling, he killed.

Every living soul is looking eternally, searching, and fighting for security. Security is the touchstone, the kernel, an important source of all human emotion and conflict.

Even the noblest of all human emotions, mother love, springs from the knowledge that her future life is insecure until her offspring are alive and propagate her kind to the end of time. Through her child a mother expects to achieve immortality, security even after her death.

Bad judgment is not necessarily the result of ignorance but if you put the case under close scrutiny, you will find that the person with bad judgment usually is ignorant of the subject concerning which he made his bad judgment.

A young woman of, say, twenty-five, works with a young man. She's good-looking; he's not. She has almost a perfect figure; he is paralyzed from the hips down. She's a stenographer; he's a young lawyer. They marry. The fact is, she proposed marriage and she was chasing after him, and not he after her. Why?

For your information, here are the facts. The man was a young struggling lawyer without any money whatsoever—and a cripple to boot. Why did she choose this cripple for marriage, instead of waiting for a healthy man with a more substantial background? Why? What was her motivation? From a distance it seems her action was against all common sense. She was not in love with the man, so what in heaven's name was her reason?

Here is the motivation. The girl came from a religious and a very conservative family. She had a widowed mother, who worked very hard to earn her living and support her only child. She took in washing, and their two-room apartment was in perpetual confusion. Wet and drying clothes hung all over the place. Even to talk about sex was evil; to practice it without marriage would bring eternal hell-fire to the sinner. The girl, to escape this monotony, poverty, and ignorance, did have affairs, first with one, then with many other men.

It was a desperate revolt against her drab life. She felt guilty and remorseful, but she had no strength to stop.

Life offered very little to her. She managed to finish high school without learning much. She was a good girl, really. She loved and helped her mother, but only through her secret excursions into sex relationships with men could she keep her sanity.

When she met the cripple in the office he shared with other lawyers, his unashamed admiration for her made her decide to marry this man. She realized that a normal man would never forgive her indiscretions, while this cripple would be happy just to have her as his wife. She knew she would be secure with this man, and that he would worship her.

There's your motivation.

Ask your friend why he married that particular girl. Or ask the girl why she married your friend. They may look at you with a smile and with great condescension say: "We got married because we love each other." But ask them further: What is love? Oh no, they won't be embarrassed, because, you see, they know all the answers, as most people do, and they will give you the old bromide—that love is a physical and spiritual attraction. People have heard this kind of questions and answers so long that they repeat them without thinking or questioning their validity.

If you want to understand motivation, and want to write good stories or plays, you had better reject such insipid surface explanations of anything.

Love is much more than physical or mental attraction. It is more than compatability—*although all this is part of the whole*. Love is my firm belief that my beloved is absolutely devoted to me and this devotion gives me confidence in myself and in my future. I want to emphasize this point. Physical attraction plus compatability plus the importance

[ 64 ]

of being important plus the belief in this person's absolute loyalty add up to love; in short, love is security.

No, you don't have to accept my definition of love, or of anything else. You can formulate your own definition; you should, anyway. You might as well know that rejection of a theory you disagree with is, if nothing else, a sign that your imagination is in working order. But be careful while in pursuit of this highly important factor in writing. Remember that there is no guarantee that imagination will carry you always in the right direction. But slavish acceptance of tradition just because it is ancient can be as detrimental and harmful as a misdirected imagination.

Some writers just waddle along like a fat goose on top of a manure heap pecking industriously away for some thought morsels someone dropped carelessly. Such writing necessarily shows poverty of mind. Such an author kills a wife in his story because of a great discovery: he, the husband, was jealous. And you can look in vain for the host of motivations that swarm around, for what *started* the chain of events which at the end culminated in murder.

The new girl in the office was delighted with the woman office manager, who turned out to be not only charming and encouraging, but actually helped her to do her job the proper way. She was flabbergasted. She thought there must be a catch somewhere. No superior had ever been as solicitous as this one. The office manager was young, about twenty-eight, very good-looking, and had poise and good manners. Everyone loved her—including the two bosses. In fact, the younger one was "going after" her in full blast. Why, then, her humility? Why wasn't she swell-headed as the managers in other offices usually were?

The new girl was very much intrigued with this strange

behavior. Why should she behave as she did? Why all this goodness? And this woman's attitude toward all the personnel in the office wasn't just a passing fancy, the new girl found out. Girls who had worked with her for years assured the new girl that she was always the same.

Why? . . . Here is the answer.

When she was twenty-two, she was caught with her parents and two brothers in a fiery inferno—their house burned down. The four others died a horrible death. She was saved, but burned so badly that the doctors considered it a miracle that she remained alive. She lived and with much plastic surgery became once more a presentable young woman who could go out and earn her living. There are always exceptions, but somehow one who once comes into such close proximity to death, as she did, learns to look at life differently than those whose lives have not been marred with horror.

Since I am talking about motivation, this brings to my mind the curious phenomenon of a man who was a coward one day, and a death-defying hero the next. I wondered what could have made him act that way.

Cowardice, as I see it, is not a permanent state. It changes with circumstances and with the moods these circumstances create. A man may walk down the street not thinking of anything special. Suddenly the shouts of passers-by attract his attention. He looks around and sees a woman crossing the street directly in the path of an oncoming speeding giant truck. The driver apparently doesn't see the woman and the woman, deep in thought, doesn't hear the rumbling of the deadly monster rushing toward her.

Our man may grasp the situation in a split second. There is no time for deliberation. He may spring forward under an impulse and push the woman out of the way—but there is no certainty that he himself might not be crushed instead.

The time between looking up and sizing up the situation to the moment of deciding whether he should help the woman or not might require perhaps not more than a millionth of a second. But in this millionth of a second a thousand living pictures of his past and present life will flash through his mind with the rapidity of light. In this infinitesimal time it will be decided whether this man will act cowardly or heroically. At the same time it will be decided whether that unknown woman shall live, whether he will risk his own life for hers.

What causes him to feel ready to exchange his very life for the life of an unknown person?

Scientists say that before the uranium atom splits, it first turns into plutonium. In the case of our man, whatever decision he makes, a preliminary mood must be created. The creation of a mood must be swift in such an emergency. The material must be there, ready, in the man, ready to explode or fizzle out. What is this mood, what are the ingredients which have the power to overwhelm a man to such an extent that he in his "mood of exaltation" is ready to sacrifice his life—when at other times he is just a plain, ordinary coward?

Let us see first the definition of cowardice. The Century Dictionary says: "Cowardice: want of courage to face danger, difficulty, opposition; dread of exposure to harm or pain of any kind."

Accepting this definition as correct, we ask why this man should create a mood for himself which will make him brave and, in consequence, possibly cause his own death. The answer is that he is powerless to create any kind of mood. The ingredients in him decide the result beforehand; necessarily it must have been in him to start with. He has nothing to do with the final decision.

The man, then, already possesses the ingredients which will create the all-powerful "mood," the mood which will be the arbiter between life and death. Let us examine these ingredients which are the core, the reason behind the action of this man—of all men.

If he happened to have a mother who for some reason or other neglected him in childhood, he might have grown into adulthood with a bitter taste in his mouth against women. And if, to top this, he has had an unfortunate love affair, was betrayed, perhaps, his resentment might have grown to such proportions that he later married for one unconscious, single purpose—to take revenge on the sex which humiliated him and made him feel unimportant.

The above conjecture might be only one of the many reasons that, while not deliberately making him condemn that woman to die before the onrushing truck, yet make him hesitate for the split second longer which spells death to her.

Remembered experiences from the past and present will create a predetermined reaction, and these, in the final analysis, will decide whether he'll appear a coward or a hero to those witnessing that particular scene.

The man who acts like a coward today may be a shining example of bravery tomorrow, for some other reason.

Motivation not only fascinates us, but it is the very essence of all great writing. Nothing ever happened or will ever happen without sound motivation.

What a miraculous spectacle it is to see the blood on its tireless, unending travel under our skin, carrying oxygen through the entire human body. But to show through your imagination and motivation how a pregnant thought can grow into determination, how determination crystallizes into action, is as miraculous as anything human ingenuity ever produced.

Motivation is to instigate; to incite to action; inducement to reason; to stimulate. Motivation can spring from many sources. One can be inspired by love; or spurred to action by hate; fanaticism will move one even to sacrifice one's life. Love for fame or for wealth are powerful instigators for action.

The basic source of all human emotion and all conflict is the eternal unquenchable thirst for safety, security, in short, for self-preservation.

# CHAPTER 9

# *Motivation—II*

## *Case Histories*

The greatest mystery on earth is man. He looks so simple, so tractable, and at the same time so unbelievably complex. He says one thing and in the next instance shamelessly contradicts himself. If you call him unreliable or unstable, he'll be mortally wounded.

He tells you, and he believes it, that he is incapable of doing any wrong—ever. He has the best of intentions. The blame must fall on the other fellow, who invariably commits all the blunders.

Don't you recognize this man? I am sure you must know at least one. He grows everywhere, like a weed. You don't? Too bad, because it is you and I, all of us—with a few exceptions. But those who admit that they too can be wrong sometimes are unnatural people, even mad. The general rule is that even if you or I make a mistake, it is really not our mistake, because, you see, on the slightest provocation we start to rationalize until we've convinced ourselves that the blame must fall on the other fellow because he influenced us first.

Why should this be so? Why must you or I be always blameless? Why must you or I be always right? Very simple. Because we are terribly insecure.

You may say, perhaps, that you are insecure, but that not everybody feels that way. I am sorry, my friend, but only mad people or idiots can live in such a happy nirvana that insecurity is a nonexistent concept.

Insecurity is the basic law of existence. All human emotion and all actions, good or evil, without any exception, spring from this one eternal source. Without insecurity there would be no progress. Life would stand still. Life would be impossible.

Security? Yes, there is such a thing too, but it is so transient that in one moment it's here and the next it's gone. You can't keep it long enough. You can't ever be bored with it, because the slightest flutter of dissonance makes it melt into thin air without a trace.

Motivation is endless—but still it can be simplified, if you accept the concept that the feeling of insecurity is one of the most important and complex of all human emotions and conflicts.

Let me see if this is true, by examining a few actual case histories I personally know about.

A man happily married, the father of three beautiful children, loved by everyone, goes out one day and commits suicide. Why? . . .

A charming young woman with a loving husband and a little genius of a boy actually throws herself at any man who wants her. Promiscuity? No. Lack of love? No. Her husband is liable to commit suicide or murder, if he finds out her infidelity, and—still she has to go with other men, even if the price be death. Why? . . .

A rich man forges a signature on a check, is arrested,

[71]

tried, and sentenced to one-year imprisonment. No financial reason made him do this. Then why did he do it?

I can go on this way endlessly, but let me look more closely at these cases first and see if my supposition that insecurity is the base of all human emotion is true or false.

Insecurity is as well disguised as neutrons and electrons are in an almost impregnable shell, the atom. Generally speaking, insecurity cannot be seen at first glance.

*Still, insecurity is at the bottom of all human action, be it good or evil.* All cowardice or heroism, all human sacrifice, happens because the authors of these deeds wish to annihilate the eternal, the indestructible menace of our life: insecurity.

There goes a man all puffed up. He plays the big shot. Dressed to kill. Big diamond pin in his necktie. He must be important. He is. And he wants the whole world to see it.

Why? Importance is the first line of defense against insecurity. But there goes another man, a very well-known man indeed, a millionaire. And he looks like an ordinary working stiff. What does he hide? He is really very important. Why doesn't he show it, like the other fellow did? Do you know the answer? Of course you do. Everyone knows how rich, how influential, how powerful he is. He doesn't want to arouse more envy and hatred than there is already. He prefers to show simplicity and minimize wealth, and hides his wealth and his shaky security behind a well-simulated simplicity.

Insecurity is very versatile. It can hide in the most improbable places. Even loyalty, the most beautiful concept, is nothing else than a hiding place, a price for security—we think we're getting love in return. But security at best is a very unstable, a very unreliable friend.

Women who wish to marry and propose to murderers must be frustrated, humiliated, and wretched individuals. They too want to feel useful, important, and have a goal to live for. All this goes for men, too, who propose marriage to murderesses.

Love, too, is a very good atom-bomb shelter in which to hide against insecurity. For our undying loyalty and love we feel, we hope, we can buy in return eternal love, which would spell security for us. But love, like everything else in life, is perishable. It changes with the passing of time and if you don't look out, undying love might turn into just the opposite—hate and death.

Yes, importance is the first line of defense. Many a time it seems or we imagine that importance is out of all proportion, like a giant electrified steel wall which can keep all evil away from us.

Yes, importance can do a lot for us. It's good for the ego, for our hope, and for our health, too, but it can capture security, the divine, the dream of all dreams, for only a very short time. You see, your importance is a very unstable commodity. Many people envy it, and many try to undermine it and destroy it.

Oh, there are many ways to make yourself important. Try humility, for instance. It works every time. Some men are parading in humility as if it were a beautiful and priceless garment.

There is a very good reason for this. Great humility makes one important. Great sacrifice will do the same. It will raise you above the head of the crowd. People feel that no price is too great for admiration, and many jeopardize their very lives to achieve it.

The man I've mentioned before, who it seemed senselessly committed suicide, in reality had many very good reasons to do away with himself. The autopsy showed that he was hopelessly sick with cancer, but for the love of his family he had kept it a secret.

But people never commit suicide for sickness alone, even if that sickness happens to be deadly. People usually cling to their lives to the bitter end. What could have been another reason?

Financial difficulty would be a very good reason and—perhaps this is the most important reason—under the surface, he knew that his "loving wife" wasn't so loving after all and she would not see him through a prolonged sickness. *Only those people commit suicide who have lost the last shred of hope.*

A candidate for suicide must have more than one reason to believe that all the claims holding him to life are gone—gone forever. So he dies, because he can't be important any more, and he is too humiliated to show himself in this pitiful and deplorable condition to those he loved. The only way out of this dilemma for him, he thinks, is death.

In death he expects to arouse compassion, tenderness, even pain, in those he cared about. And at the price of his life he'll make himself once more, for the last time, important.

And now there is the young wife who throws herself to any man who wants her, while courting murder and suicide. Why? It is a pitiful tale to tell. She feels that she, as a woman, is a total flop. Her figure, as she explains haltingly, never developed as it should have. She has very small breasts. But she's good-looking, chic, and charming. What more can anyone want?

Didn't her husband marry her? No, he didn't, she tells me.

"I went after him, courted him, pleased him. I gave

myself to him as an inducement, played the virgin when I wasn't, flattered him, built up his ego, helped him in his business. Made myself indispensable—and now . . ."

"And now, you're indispensable to him," I said. "What else do you want?"

"I want to be like other women. I die from sheer envy when I see a girl or a woman with a full bosom. The bosom is the beauty, the glory of a woman, a sign of fertility . . ."

"You have a wonderful body . . ."

"Men don't desire me as they do other women. I want to be desired . . ." She cried . . ., "I know I am no good and I'm going from one bed to another, looking for the assurance that I am every bit as desirable as any other woman."

"When you make a conquest, why aren't you satisfied?" I asked. "How can I be?" she answered bitterly. "Why not?" "Because the men I give myself to are never the kind a woman would be proud of. They might have pitied me . . . or perhaps I wooed them, instead of their wooing me . . . as it should be . . . oh God, I am not a woman . . ."

And she cried and cried. There was a tragedy because she couldn't be as important as any common everyday (ordinary) woman could, without any effort on her part. She wasn't important, and to achieve a modicum of stability in her own mind—she risked a human life.

Would you call her a bad woman? No, not I; I wouldn't. She's just an unfortunate person, thrown into the arms of the blackest, the cruelest, and seemingly the most eternal insecurity.

I hasten to add that not all flat-chested women try to establish their lost equilibrium with an always new and exciting male, served to them at bedtime. But one thing is certain, and that is that anyone with a deficiency will

[ 75 ]

try to compensate with some kind of mastery in a profession or in a subject.

I mentioned before, and I'll do it over and over again, that there are no living beings who are wholly satisfied with themselves. *Ergo,* we're all looking for some kind of compensation. The differences between people lie in the severity of their own shortcomings.

And the degree of dissatisfaction with oneself will be determined by our physical make-up and our immediate environment. Hypersensitivity over the slightest disapproval usually springs from a weak body with a low physical resistance.

I am sure you know a few similar cases yourself. Of course you do. I remind you that a big nose, or big feet or hands, or lack of hair, or too much hair, or a bad kidney, or varicose veins on a girl's leg make any one of those people the victim of the most insidious of diseases: Fear.

As you know, fear is the loving son of insecurity. They are inseparable . . . they might as well be the Siamese twins. They are the real Siamese twins.

I know a young girl who committed suicide because one of her ankles was thicker than the other one, and there was no money in the house to finance an operation. She had no ambition and she had no other outlet for her imagination to work on. So that thick ankle of hers apparently meant life and death to her. But let us never forget that no one ever commits suicide for one reason only, but for a variety of reasons. In this case the thick ankle of hers was only the last, the very last, straw. And this slight deficiency tipped the scales in favor of death.

Whether people know it or not, they look constantly for an outlet for their talent, to succeed, to better themselves, to be noticed, to be important. Great ambition is usually a compensation for some deficiency in the person. Most of the great men of the world became great for that very reason, because there was something wrong with them.

Remember the man who forged the signature and let himself be jailed? I am sure you know now why he did such a stupid thing. Didn't he know what was going to happen to him if he was caught? Of course he did. He did it to be caught. Can you guess why he did it? Insecurity, yes. But will he be more secure in jail than out of it? Of course not.

I told you before, insecurity hides in the most impossible places. In this man's case, he did forge that signature deliberately, because his family looked at him as a walking and living meal ticket.

He complained many times that nobody cared for him any more. They laughed in his face and told him, "Of course we love you, Pop," and promptly forgot him again. Forging that signature was a trick to punish them and to shake them out of their complacency. He wanted to be noticed, he wanted to be the center of interest once more.

This man's action cannot be characterized as a stroke of genius. It simply indicated that poor man's mental and physical ability and nothing more. Another man in his place might have acquired some kind of a hobby. Another might have gone overboard for women. It all depends on the individual involved.

I wish to emphasize over and over again that all human emotion and conflict originates from this one and only source: insecurity.

# CHAPTER 10

# *Motivation—III*

## I

### Environment

There is a reason—a motivation, that is—for every move we make. Motivation can come from a dream, a quarrel, from eating a good meal, a disappointment—or, for that matter, from anywhere under the sun. But we can and must trace all the milliard motivations to their origin.

The sources of all motivations are the *physical make-up* of a person and his *environment*. His sensitivity or his brutality, his attitude toward himself and toward the world, is shaped by the above-mentioned two sources.

Let me test this to see if it is true.

Some time ago I read a newspaper account of how an eleven-year-old shoeshine boy, Paul, by name, innocently caused the death of another shoeshine boy. It was a pitiful story.

The father of Paul had been killed in an accident. His widow was left with her own three children from a previous marriage. They were left without funds, and Paul decided that shining shoes would bring in more money than running errands or delivering newspapers, so he built a wooden box and selected a busy corner in the Bronx, not far from his home. He thought he was ready for business. He was ready, all right, but the fellow whose place he had innocently taken had different and violent ideas about Paul's sudden and unannounced competition.

When he arrived and saw a stranger in his usual place, he attacked Paul without asking questions or giving him a chance to explain. In his rightful indignation he administered a bloody beating upon poor Paul.

Paul resisted at first, but finding the other fellow too strong for him, broke away and ran. In the ensuing chase the other boy was run over and killed instantly by a truck.

This was the story I read. Part of the motivation, as usual, came from the sordid environment the boys were living in. Now, I want to see what I can do with the meager information the newspapers have given me.

The following is the result of my imagination. Please note that I shall try to build a sound motivation—which springs from his environment—for every move my character is going to make.

The investigation into the death of Robert Remete, aged thirteen, took almost three weeks, but Paul was cleared of guilt. It was established beyond the shadow of a doubt that Robert had been crushed to death by a truck as he was chasing Paul.

Not long afterwards, Paul appeared once more at the same subway station with his shoeshine box. The best place was just beside the candy store, which commanded a strategic position where the boys could try to catch the eye of a prospective customer. This was the envied spot of bullying Robert Remete, but after his death the next in line, Chiko Marossa, a dark, tall, lanky boy, took it over as his rightful legacy. Nobody dared to contradict him.

He was a tough boy, and the others readily accepted him as the arbiter in all their disputes. On the memorable morning that Paul again appeared on the scene, he, being the first, took his position before the candy store. That had been Robert Remete's place, and Paul had naïvely concluded that since he was dead, the place must be empty and naturally there would be no dispute if he took it for himself. So he put his shoeshine box on the sidewalk and stood behind it, leaning against the red brick wall, ready for business.

Paul had come back to the same place instead of going somewhere else because he already knew a few of the boys in the neighborhood, and besides, in stubborn rebellion, he felt that he was entitled to stay any place he wished. The real motivation behind his determination to come back to this place was that he felt at home here already and knew this neighborhood better than any other. If worst came to worst, he could escape new pursuers with much greater ease than before.

As the day wore on, the other boys began to arrive. They looked at Paul with amazement and moved further on without saying a word to him. "Gee," one boy said, "What noive!" This kid had caused the death of the toughest fellow in town, and now he had come back for more. What a baby! The boys' eyes held fear and respect for Paul, both powerful deterrents from being chummy with him. They had seen him give a good account of himself in the fight with the roughneck. He is dangerous, they thought, and left him alone.

Paul watched the boys' guarded faces and knew there would be trouble again. He started to shiver inside. He felt as though millions of ants were crawling all over his body.

"Shine, mister?" he cried, and he didn't recognize his own voice. It was husky and throaty. Once he'd had an inflammation of the throat and could hardly talk. He felt the same lump now as then, obstructing the free passage of air.

"Shine? Shine, mister?" No one was passing just then, but he hollered anyway. It showed courage. It said to the boys, "I'm here to stay! What are ya gonna do about it!"

He remembered his stepmother's tearful eyes, begging him to take care of himself when he had left in the morning. He had promised and hurried away, because he was afraid he might burst out crying. He felt like crying right now. He wanted to bury his head in his stepmother's ample bosom, as he had done many times before. She loved him, and in sheer tenderness she used to squeeze him to herself. Paul felt so happy at such moments that he wanted that feeling to stay with him the rest of his life.

Whenever he thought of this strange feeling toward his stepmother, he felt guilty and ashamed. There was something mysterious and brave in this feeling. He was challenging these boys right now because of it. A quiet voice said within him, "You could go somewhere else, you know," but he knew that to obey it would be cowardly. It would mean betraying the trust of his stepmother.

"Shine! Shine, mister!" As he looked up, he saw Chiko Marossa, the roughneck, the boy whose place he had unknowingly usurped, standing before him. The boy's dark face became darker as he looked at Paul. Paul gasped as he missed a heartbeat, and in that breathless moment he decided he wouldn't run away even if he must die. He cried his defiance once more: "Shine, mister!" Then he looked deliberately at Chiko and said, "Do you want somethin'?"

Chiko felt like smashing Paul's face, but he had been present at the funeral of his best friend. He had seen the peace of eternity on the yellow face. And now, as he looked at Paul, he recalled sickeningly that this skinny slob was the cause of his friend's death. Chiko shivered as terror started to rattle his legs. A nameless fear gripped him and, without answering Paul, he walked away with his shoe-shine box.

## II

I have always wanted to see how "environment" influences people, molding them into new shapes. I have always wanted to stand face to face with this overbearing, all-powerful monster, who can accomplish the impossible. He is the undisputed ruthless, uncompromising Caesar of man. I've always wanted to know whether man submits or fights against this tyranny. What chance has he to escape from its bondage? What weapons can he use against this paralyzing "influence of environment"?

Let me see. I think I know Paul quite well. I'll try to build a background for him. I know he defied a cruel beating because of his love for his stepmother. She gave him what he has never had before—his role of savior with the other children, his self-respect, his awakening manhood, the lure of making money, the fascination of seeing the world, the always exciting, new, and sometimes grotesque panorama of experiences he calls fun, and finally, greater security.

Right now, Paul is a nice boy. He is brave at the moment because cowardice would bring hunger, shame, and loss of the adoration of his brothers and sisters and the tenderness of his stepmother.

He is really frightened, but the boys on the street are afraid of him. The tough guy who wanted to kill him a few weeks ago now really (with his dead body), in his death, is protecting Paul from further harm. The memory of Robert's untimely death is a monument to Paul's invincibility. The conception of death is actually vague to these boys. It doesn't mean dissolution, dust to dust, as far as they are concerned. They know the boy is dead and buried, but the important thing is that this tough has made it impossible for him to come back to his usual haunts. Because of him, Robert is in the cemetery, and the boys remember how they hate to go near a cemetery, even in the daytime.

So now, there stands Paul, with the mysterious and invisible "influence of environment" all around him. Although it can't be seen, it is working on him constantly. He is standing there, up to his neck in the environment, like a man standing on the bottom of the ocean with just water, water, all around him and above him.

Now let us see how Paul is going to be influenced. But I must remember that environment is not constituted only of people. It is also houses, the streets he lives in and walks on. Even gasoline fumes, strange as it may seem, belong to environment.

Environment is everywhere. It is the gray sky, and it is present downtown, in stuffy apartments, on the fifth floor of a tenement. The crying babies, the cursing mothers, the drunken fathers, also belong, and perhaps they build a horror in you against squalling babies with eternally dirty, running noses. I must remember the food Paul eats, his father and his real mother, the grocery store flat where

[ 83 ]

he was conceived and then born, everything living and dead, all the noises he ever heard, all the smells he ever smelled, the lights and shadows, and the bedbugs in the beds, for all these are environment. Even the dreams he dreamed, the thoughts he thought, are a part of the whole and of him.

So there stands Paul, with his shoeshine box, and he would never believe it if someone were to tell him that he too is a part of environment for others. But he is, and slowly he realizes that the boys are genuinely afraid of him. This realization takes time, of course. At last Paul lets go of fear, which he has been clutching desperately for so long, and gradually starts to expand. His face loses its hunted look. His breathing becomes more normal. He starts to talk more freely to the boys, and later when he sees that they are still afraid of him, he becomes more authoritative.

Paul has no way of knowing that the transition in him was brought about by the influence of his environment. The environment never said to Paul, "From now on you can bully these boys. They are afraid of you." Environment never talks. Its ways are the most subtle on earth. It is not even a whisper, or a feeble sigh of dying. It is not a shadow. Environment is a monster one day and a savior the next. Environment is in the air, it is the air itself, it is stone, and it is human flesh. Environment speaks without speaking. It grows in you as the grass grows, soundlessly.

Without knowing how it had happened, Paul developed an appetite for money, easy money. He came to know certain types of people intimately. There was a fellow, for instance, with an enormous stomach. He weighed three hundred pounds if he weighed one; his trousers always seemed to be on the verge of falling off. When Paul shined his shoes, the big fellow couldn't see him because of his blown-up belly. Paul laughingly thought it was just like an umbrella; you could hide under it and never get wet in a downpour, not in a thousand years.

He was fun, this guy Rudolpho. He liked to laugh, and Paul was fascinated watching the way that jellylike barrel started to shake, as if someone was tickling it from inside. Then all that fat would suddenly jump into the air, as if it wanted to find a new place for itself right under Rudolpho's chin. Then it seemed to fall down to his very knees, then up again and down, up and down, and it was like a miracle the way that drumlike thing acted as if it had a separate life of its own. When Rudolpho decided to go anywhere, first his stomach started to shake, then move, and he simply followed his own stomach.

This Rudolpho fellow was in the numbers racket. He hated moving around to see all the people he had to see, so he began taking Paul with him to do the leg-work. Paul was willing because Rudolpho was generous. For a couple of hours' work, Rudolpho gave him one, two, sometimes three dollars, depending upon his mood and intake.

Paul would have laughed his head off if somebody had told him that, from the moment Rudolpho appeared on the horizon of his life, the big man had become a part of his environment and was going to exert an immense influence on him from then on.

Rudolpho was a small-time racketeer. He lived on other fellows as a louse lives on living things, and he tried to chisel for himself on the side. His job was taking bets and paying out on the rare times that some lucky bastard hit the right number. But Rudolpho wasn't satisfied with his take, and slowly tried to build up a clientele for himself. He knew that if he were caught by the big fellows he might be taken for a ride, but he thought that since he acted decently to the people he dealt with, they would never give him away.

But there is always a leak somewhere, and one day when Paul went to see him in his two-room bachelor apartment, he was surprised to see the door half open. Paul was justly surprised because Rudolpho was a very cautious man. He had a chain and two Yale locks on his half-rotten door, and he would never, not even for a second, leave it open. He lived in constant fear. His apartment was on West 110th Street. His door was in a dark hallway just off the stoop, in a half-empty, condemned house, a firetrap if there ever was one. Rudolpho had lived there alone for many years, cooking and cleaning for himself.

Paul felt uneasy, seeing that half-open door. He pushed it cautiously and called out, "Rudolpho, are you there?" There was no answer. The window shades were down, and it was almost black in the room. Paul stepped in and called again, but at the same instant he saw Rudolpho sitting in the middle of the room at a table, staring at him.

"You bastard," Paul said out loud, laughing. "You wanted to scare me, didn't you?"

He went to the behemoth man sitting on his enormous behind and started to give him a friendly poke in the ribs, but stopped, startled. He saw that the grin on that face was frozen into a yellow wax. On his white shirt was the zig-zag of dried blood. Rudolpho was dead, all right, and the spectacle of him sitting there with sightless eyes, looking at Paul and grinning, was the most ghastly sight Paul had ever seen in all his life.

Environment is only a part—a very large part, to be sure —of ready-made motivation. In fact, environment is like a big, comfortable bed, waiting for us the moment we are born.

However, as our mental horizon widens, our environment becomes uncomfortable, but fear of the unknown still keeps us glued to the now despised but familiar place.

Without *environment,* no one can create a living three-dimensional character.

# CHAPTER 11

# Motivation—IV

### The Story of an Ugly Man

This will be the story of an ugly man who killed because *he thought* he was ugly. In the previous chapter we were witnessing *environment* in action.

Now motivation again will help environment and its twin brother, physical make-up, to mold or rather twist a human being into a grotesque shape.

The following is an excerpt from a local newspaper:

## WIFE KILLER SURRENDERS

## MOST BRUTAL MURDER IN THE ANNALS OF OUR TIME

## WIFE'S FACE UNRECOGNIZABLE

## HE DID IT, HE CLAIMS, BECAUSE HE LOVED HER

"Mr. Guy Smith was arrested last night for the brutal murder of his beautiful wife, Anne. Mr. Smith's arrest came as a complete shock to the community. He was known as an even-tempered, fair-minded citizen, member of the local section of the Rotary Club and generous supporter of many worthy and charitable causes."

Then the paper went into the gory details of how they found Mrs. Smith's mutilated body, what time the murder occurred, how Mr. Smith surrendered to the police. He was calm, even serene, police reported. The fact is that Mr. Smith called the police himself. Then with the utmost self-possession, he sat down in a rocking-chair and waited for his arrest.

Smith was not only willing to admit the murder, but explained to the astonished district attorney how he had planned to kill his wife. This confession made the murder a premeditated one and Smith a candidate for the electric chair.

According to the psychiatrist, Smith was absolutely sane and responsible for his act. They pointed out to him that he had the legal right *not to answer* any questions which might implicate him, but Smith almost eagerly volunteered to give all the information, all the data which would help him to be executed as quickly as possible.

In prison he was not even downhearted. He was jovial, seemed absolutely relaxed as if he had no care in the world.

Why should a seemingly healthy person wish to die? The normal reaction is to escape punishment, even if one has committed a crime.

In Smith's case, his physical make-up was a very strong motivation in making him morbidly sensitive. He wasn't deformed or disgustingly ugly. He was just not the type one would call good-looking. His face was shallow, his nose broken, and his eyes were somehow always inflamed.

No, he wasn't exactly ugly, but unfortunately he thought

he was, and this conviction of his made him what he became: a killer.

Now let us see how all this transformation came about.

This man Smith was a tolerably intelligent man. He had never been a mental giant, but when he compared himself to others, the result was very disheartening. His hypersensitiveness and his unruly imagination made him see things that weren't there.

Let us remember that this man killed his wife. We want to understand what tragic evolution made him do this.

Who knows our limitations better than ourselves? To know how little one knows is a bitter pill for a sensitive person to swallow. Smith knew how limited he was in his profession. He was an accountant. A free-lancer. Furthermore, *he was painfully aware that as a human specimen he could not, by any stretch of the imagination, be called an Adonis.*

His constant fear of losing his beloved wife made him kow-tow to her, which, after a while, made him actually repulsive to her. His politeness and his eagerness to please increased, if possible, instead of diminishing.

This self-abasement went so far that it gave Mrs. Smith physical anguish to be near him. He was good twenty-four hours a day, and his behavior made it harder for her to come to a conclusion. She planned to leave him. He, on the other hand, sensing that his value was decreasing at an alarming rate, desperately tried to recoup the esteem that he had lost through the years.

He began giving her expensive gifts which he could not afford. (He accepted bribes to falsify income-tax returns.) He tried to transform himself from a middle-aged man into a young, vivacious one. He started to prance around, flirting with young women, making himself utterly ridiculous. His plan to make his wife jealous was so transparent that, instead of being angry, she actually encouraged his escapades, thinking that perhaps this way she could get rid of him sooner.

His expensive gifts were not appreciated. His wife felt an even greater need to escape. The tension grew between them, yet neither uttered a word about what was uppermost in their minds. The unbearable atmosphere had to explode, shattering all the make-believe, lies, and hypocrisy.

At last the truth came out—she wanted a divorce. And for the first time Smith consciously was pushed toward murder. For the first time, he thought his wife should be dead. This thought was not born of frenzy. It was a logical step and he, in horror, was repelled by it at almost the moment it was born.

In the first split second that this idea came into being, he knew that, with her death, he must die too. And he was not ready for that ultimate decision—yet.

The idea of killing someone is much more satisfying to entertain than that of seeing oneself as a corpse. This understandable love of life makes cowards of us all. Smith tried to figure out how he could stay alive. In his desperation he lost the last shred of human dignity. He begged, he threatened. Nothing mattered any more. He fought only for the humiliating privilege of being near her.

Did she allow him? She did, for various reasons. First, she really pitied him. Secondly, if he had seen that her determination is inexorable, he might have slowly gotten used to the idea. Still another reason: since she told him that living with him was out of the question, she felt free to go out with other men, hoping Smith would reconcile himself to the inevitable.

[ 91 ]

And the most important reason of all: before leaving him she intended to collect half the price of their home— a six-family house in which she was part owner.

Smith was originally a kind, mellow man. The thought of murder must have grown slowly in his head. What kind of provocation must have exploded in his mind to have forced him to make that last fatal step, which ended not only his victim's life but also his own?

Smith had asked only one privilege, that she let him stay. Feeling sorry for him, she agreed, and with this act she started a chain of reactions which culminated in her own death.

Again, the provocation must have been great. Strange men would come to *his* house. This was betrayal in his eyes. What right had she to defile his home?

Perhaps she never entertained the idea of bringing men into the house, but her actions may have suggested that she did.

He felt he could not go on thinking these thoughts. It was worse than the punishment promised to the blackest sinner in hell. But still he hoped she would come back to him. Why?

How in heaven's name could a man like Smith think, even for a moment, that everything might turn out for the best? Was there any possibility of this? None at all. Then, why did he delude himself with false hopes? For a very good reason: this hope must have meant more to him than marital happiness—more than anything in the world. *It meant his life.*

This woman, when she met him, made him believe that he *belonged;* that he was *as good as anyone else, or better.* She made him believe in human dignity. She gave him the all-important feeling that he was wanted, that he was important, really important, and then she was ready to destroy all the *self-confidence* she built up in him.

This catastrophe had to be prevented at all costs. To him, her desire to leave meant deceit, betrayal. It seemed that, when they first met, she lied to him about his prowess and his looks. Now a divorce would certainly make him the laughingstock of all who knew him.

Divorce to him had much more significance than it would have to others. It meant, in his case, that he would be left unprotected in the midst of a hostile world. Divorce meant losing the one thing that kept him alive—the security of marriage.

If she had lied when she said he was good, then his own previous estimate of himself *was right, and later it was conclusively proved that he was an inferior person who had no right to live.*

Mrs. Smith's request for a divorce at this stage was to him tantamount to a polite announcement, "Look, Smith, you have lived enough; it is time you lie down peacefully and die."

A divorce meant death to Smith. That is why he became desperate. He fought for his life, and when he lost hope of saving it, he killed—in self-defense, according to his topsy-turvy reasoning.

Smith was not mad. We would not be interested in him if he were. But we become increasingly excited as we observe him sliding irrevocably into desperation and chaos.

Whether one has a physical handicap or not, the important thing is what the individual thinks of himself. If he feels he is not exactly a bargain, it is a nearly impossible task to make him think otherwise.

[ 93 ]

The second most important motivation for human behavior is our own physical make-up.

Yes, it is true, but without humiliation in childhood, neglect, and abuse, or love and tenderness, no character can be a totally distressing pessimist or a smiling optimist.

A three-dimensional human being is not only influenced by his environment, but his physical make-up as well.

This man Smith must have had more than his share of humiliation in childhood to feel as he did about his looks.

CHAPTER 12
_____

# *Imagination at Work*

Persons afflicted with color blindness, try as they might to be painters or artists, must fail for obvious reasons. Common sense also dictates that a deaf person should not try to be a concert violinist.

But what about persons with faulty imagination who aspire to be writers? The question is not how great is their handicap but whether or not it can be overcome. While color blindness cannot be cured, imagination can positively be improved.

Science can measure heights, depths, intelligence, and the complicated functions of the mechanism of the human mind. However, I have never heard of any meter which can read or measure the strength and intensity of the imagination. If you intend to become a sportsman, you can test your body resistance under hammer blows of prolonged exercise. Unfortunately a writer has no such concrete blueprint with which to test the strength or intensity of his imagination.

I have talked to many persons who wanted to become writers. Their intelligence and imagination were in perfect order. But when they began to write a story or play, their intelligence and imagination played tricks on them. They refused to function properly!

These people had imagination. But they didn't know how to control it. It bounced them around like an untamed colt! Imagination must be harnessed and directed. Imagination must serve its master's bidding. It is a hard process to harness and direct imagination, but it must be done. Your imagination must be released in small doses first, then developed gradually to the highest magnitude.

Learn to flip it on like a three- or six-way light bulb, yourself always in control, with one hand on the switch.

Let me give you an example:

Let us suppose that you are a member of a respected middle-class family. You live in a small community. You are a single man of twenty-five. You are in love with a wonderful girl, but need money badly to entertain her. She has not decided whether or not she will marry you! Matters are complicated by another young man who is also courting your sweetheart. You know it is expedient that you impress her with your generosity.

What will you do if you haven't any money? Are you desperate enough to get it unlawfully? Figure it out; can you do this without anyone detecting you?

Can you put yourself into this young man's precarious position? Remember, you must love this girl desperately to want to steal for her.

Now, if you decide to do this mental gymnastic, don't try to substitute any imaginary young man in your place. It must be you. I want you to be that young man, to be the one who will jeopardize your own and your family's name, and no one else. It must be your own social position, your own future at stake. Can you do all this? Of course you can. Try it.

Another mental gymnastic! Can you remember what color, shape, or style dress that your mother or sweetheart was wearing yesterday? Usually people don't remember such trivialities. But you must.

Another effective way to exercise your imagination is this. Do you know someone you detest utterly? Your hatred for this person should not be hazy or vague. It should be substantial. Your reasons for abhorring that person should be so crystal clear that you would wish him to drop dead. If you know such a person, then you have a wonderful opportunity to exercise your imagination.

The exercise will make you see *his* side of the affair. *Justify him!* Most persons believe they can't do any wrong. To them the fault always lies with the other fellow. In your case I am sure your enemy feels you are the guilty one. Can you make yourself see yourself through *his* eyes, *guilty?* Can you exonerate him from all blame? Can you imagine that he was right from start to finish?

Can you do this exercise? Can you do it so convincingly that this man's actions would appear justified? If you can, then you have given your imagination an excellent workout.

Here is an exercise by one of my students. He tried to justify the person he seemingly despised.

Did he succeed?

### Exercise for Dec. 13

Elaine O'Brien justifies in particular her firing of one Amelita Brace.

Dec. 28, 1951

Henrietta Darling,

Last month's letter was all about my relatives. Moving to the Village has me all disorganized, so this is going to be mostly about the office and my getting away from the darn place for a spell. Note the new address: 45 W. 3rd St., near the Scanlons and their lively crowd. No chance for bird-watching and skiing there, of course; but what a peachy place I'm setting up—actually, and get this, a man-trap to the best of my amateur ability, dear. So have a good laugh at me at last—for the first time in my life I'm really in circulation. I can just hear you say, "Will wonders never cease!"

I am going on a winter vacation for a starter—in the Green Mountains, of all places. Right in my bitter gall bladder is where I want to feel the bitter cold. It's a bitter thing anyway to be pitied by your bosses for your decades of efficient work. Here's the lowdown: Dr. Merriam got a plea through the board for a paid winter vacation for me, because the office would go to pieces without me, they said. That's something they didn't have to tell me.

While I am gone, the third floor is going to be in a turmoil because I'm letting my so-called second assistant go—Amelita Brace. I'll have to admit she's top-notch when she's actually busy; by the way, I told you about her—the little bitch that trumpeted a grammatical slip of mine all over the organization. But honestly, darling, I'm justified. They're going to say it's for one or all of these things: (1) for her being a raving beauty that I hate because she's a fairly good worker when she wants to be; (2) for her income topping mine I'll bet. By the way she takes orders for cheap jewelry from practically everybody; (3) for my voting with the high mucky-mucks to fire Ben Terwilliger (her boy friend, not that I knew that at the time) less for his having started the cheap jewelry game than for general inefficiency; (4) for her having called me, they

told me later, "a man-hating old bootlicker"; and (5) for
her getting a million passes a day on company time from
these dopey pipsqueaks they call the hopeful young men
at the office. No, darling. It's on account of her simply
hating my guts because I didn't requisition for her a new
leather-backed chair like the others there, and a big desk
lamp like the others. Good heavens, the outfit at her desk
was all only a year old, but she's been practically snarling
in my face about this every day. Besides, that dopey Cleo-
patra persisted over my protests in adding and adding to
my dictation work with the scads of ifs and buts she's
been writing to customers; and Jim—the elevator man, you
remember—told me the office was always in an uproar
whenever I stepped out of it for a second, with her starting it every time. And I've overlooked plenty other things
too.

Incidentally, Millington—you remember the old fool,
he was sweet on you at one time—backed up the girl
when he left; he had the dirty nerve to say that he was
resigning because I don't know how to treat the girls right
—him with his eye on that fat Costerman job for the long-
est time. And besides all this, she's been working on that
Morrison girl—my first assistant—she's been in training,
you might say, for my job before the Brace wench came,
and has a degree in journalism and public relations or
something. But due to Amelita she keeps beefing about
the work and tells everybody how bored she is under me.
What a way to start ten or fifteen years of working into
my job! I thought she had more sense. Honestly, darling,
in our office at least, the girls either get married fast or
sit around and boil about my efficiency. I was brought up
to be patient with the experienced judgment of my supe-

riors, and that's how I got my start. Who do those little would-be office-running bastards think they are, anyway?

So you see, if I don't fire her, the mucky-mucks will say I don't know how to conduct an office. You don't find me throwing my job on nasty little Cleopatras and their pipsqueak b.f.'s.

I've been wanting to write you this letter for ever so long. With me moving, you'll want, of course, to know more about dad. Well, the old coot is in an old coots' home at last. He finally admitted it was his own idea; you heard him talk about it once yourself. Before he left he nearly broke a leg falling out of a chair while asleep after opening a can of pears at three in the morning against doctor's orders. That sort of thing I could stand—but, oh God! what he started to tell one evening. He'd never mentioned anything like that before. He began it all by saying, with company present, that every time he thought about the sins of his youth, he couldn't help laughing. That did it, darling, after all the horribly strict bringing-up I got from him and mother. Why the Sam Hill didn't he ever blurt out confessions like that while I was in pigtails? Then and there, I'm telling you, something snapped between him and me—not exactly my respect for the old boy; but, after that bolt from the blue, half a century of worshiping him involuntarily—it just snapped. What I now want is for life to give me back a little of that long worship, and I'm sure you understand. Darling, you've got to!

I'm crying so hard I can hardly see the typewriter. Me an old bootlicker because I try to effect essential economies in office equipment, and a man-hater because disrupting pipsqueaks don't belong in well-run offices!

My only hope for happiness is advice from you. All of a sudden, you're almost a sort of parent to me in my thoughts, darling. I who have nurtured all these years a sort of tolerant, almost pitying and patronizing attitude toward you, as you very well knew! Well, now I want to crawl to you on my hands and knees and learn—you sweet old frantic chick, you! Bewitching men with your ringlets of snow for years and years! Naturally, I'm past all the worry I had when Jack propositioned me eleven years ago. Honestly, dear, things ought to turn out as wonderful for me at fifty-two as for you at fifty-five. Help me, darling. You thumb your pretty nose at all kinds of indifference but not the way my father did that night. So, to me, you're life and, yes, *men*—and old pop is only death and cackling memories of dead floozies. I'm not patience on a monument any more. Thank Heaven for a sweet, wonderful example like you. Science seems to have landed the world in fear; my efficiency is going to land me in hopelessness if I don't get help from you. So plan to hurry that Eastern trip soon, darling! Because I honestly never expected to say such a thing as this in all my life—I'm getting me a man *on any terms*. How horribly wonderful!

So, as usual, Happy New Year, and as usual, good luck, and as usual, Love, Elaine O'Brien

After reading this letter one feels that the author must have known just such people as he was writing about. I asked him if this was so. He said yes, he did know those people.

This proves what writers have always known: that good writing is the result of dealing with characters they themselves know best.

Good writing is more psychological *detective work* than anything else. You are not only supposed to report a deed but to understand it and analyze it to the best of your ability. Readers of today demand to know the motives behind the atrocities people commit. For commonplace reporting the public reads the newspapers, not books.

The book-reading public wants more than reporting; it wants to know what impulse, what inner force caused the catapulting of a character into a seemingly senseless adventure.

Even in a mediocre book the writer tried to the best of his ability to depict the working of his character's mind, but failed. Why? He failed because he didn't know any better. He didn't know any better because his imagination was retarded, warped, and undernourished. It never had a chance to grow up.

*Doubt* is a sign of imagination.

*Curiosity* is food for imagination.

*Foresight* is imagination.

*Understanding and Humility* are the product of superior imagination.

*Ignorance and Cruelty* are the signs of warped imagination.

Many of our writers and authors are simply reporters of events. They haven't the imagination to be anything else. To look for and to find motivation in an act is a sign of a healthy and vigorous imagination.

A married woman runs away with another man; is she a bad woman? If we examine the matter more closely, we might find dozens of reasons. Reasons, convictions not of her guilt, but of her husband's. His stupidity, neglect, insolence, and cruelty actually drove this woman into another man's arms.

Without imagination you'll never find enough motivation even to scare a fly away from your nose. Let me prove the creativeness of imagination. Let me show you how imagination really works.

How can you depend upon your imagination, especially if you're in a tight spot? My mind is a blank for the present. I am leafing through a newspaper lazily. Before I realize what is happening I find myself absorbed in a long article about a playwright who made a terrific hit last week.

For days I have been reading fantastic stories about this man and his new play. All the critics agree that he is the most promising and spectacular new find this year. There is a picture of him in the newspapers, too. I notice that he is well-built and good-looking. He's young. He's happily married. He has everything.

I scrutinized the picture thoroughly and decided that there wasn't any story there. I was about to turn the page when my eye caught a bedraggled figure in the picture with the author as he was about to step into his Cadillac. There was no connection between the absurd-looking figure and the author. I knew, however, that there was a story here, the exact nature of which I still did not know.

I have maintained that there's no story without a unity of opposites between characters. There wasn't any unity of opposites between the shabby individual and the successful author, unless that man wasn't a stranger. Now, my imagination is at work. I've made this stranger a janitor in the apartment house of the author. That would throw these two together. Now I try to establish a real unity between them.

The janitor, whom I will name Tony, is an amiable, humble person. Why should he be humble? you might ask. Because most of these people are subservient, due to the fact that their livelihood depends on the generosity of the tenants. But this does not necessarily mean that Tony should be humble too. There are haughty janitors with all types of temperaments. But for my purpose just now we will make Tony humble.

Tony has a good word for everyone. He's democratic and talkative, but unfortunately for him, no one has either the time or the inclination to exchange words or ideas with him.

I don't intend to write anything extraordinary or fantastic about these two people. I am interested only in what could actually or naturally happen to two entirely different individuals, living in different worlds socially. I can acquire this information if I unleash my imagination and direct it on its course.

Could Tony arouse the playwright's interest in his personal problem? Not just now. The playwright is a real guy, but too occupied with his own troubles. He created a stir with his play last year, and now he must outdo himself with his most recent one, or he will hear "for whom the bell tolls."

A tyro might think that once an author or playwright establishes himself he can lean back and rest on his laurels. That is a misconception. Instead, he must dive deeper into his imagination and come up with more ingenuity of daring, or he will be name-tagged a has-been or an *homme-finis!*

What situation, what force, can bring these two together?

I will tell you. If you have ever witnessed the feverish and mad preparations for a theater premiere when everything seems to go wrong, you'll understand a playwright's sudden sympathy for all the unhappy and downtrodden people of the earth.

Two days before the premiere the author felt that his play would flop. It sounded stupid to him at rehearsals. How could they have bought it, he wondered! If only he had the courage to drown himself or run away. Well, your author did neither, but two days before the premiere he did do something unusual. As he was about to slink away unseen into his apartment, he heard Tony's friendly voice.

"Good afternoon, Mr. D. It's a scorcher, isn't it?"

The author wanted to answer him abruptly as usual and duck, but instead he looked twice at the little soot-covered man and answered good afternoon. He surprised himself by the warmth in his voice as he asked Tony, "How's everything with you, my friend?"

Tony answered politely, although reservedly, the author's questions about how long he had been in the country, how many children he had, and was he happy with his wife? Tony didn't think much of the last question; it made him suspicious. The author was good-looking and Tony's wife, Maria, was beautiful, and—a flirt.

The author stepped closer to Tony and in a confidential tone asked him if he liked the theater, plays particularly. He did? Well, that was opportune! Wouldn't he like to attend a play premiere on Friday? He would? Splendid! The author gave two passes to Tony and withdrew.

The author was positive that he had gained at least one person in this cold world who would like his show, if no one else; at least Tony would be grateful.

The two days passed. Then an unbelievable and unprecedented success for the author.

The little janitor, of course, was forgotten until a week after the premiere. The author was on his way to a banquet given in his honor by the "Literary Juveniles of

America" when the gutteral accent of the little janitor caught his attention.

"Too big humidity, isn't it, Mr. D?"

"Yes," said the now-noted playwright with a tolerant smile and condescending manner. He asked the grimy one how he liked the play? The author anticipated cheers and bravos for an answer.

Instead, Tony shrugged his shoulders and said to the shocked surprise of the author, "No like 'em!"

"You don't? You didn't!" gasped the author incredulously. "Didn't you see my picture in all the newspapers?" he asked defensively. Here he stood, the janitor a comic figure, and he, the great author acclaimed by all the critics, trying to convince an ignorant janitor of his greatness. What nonsense!

"What's wrong with my play?" he demanded in a highly indignant voice. The janitor, frightened by the stir he had created in the man, was silent. But the threatening and persistent questioning of the angry author brought out a stuttered blurting from Tony. "I don't know, honest, I don't know."

The playwright assured Tony that he wasn't angry, he only wished to know what was wrong with the play . . . was it boring or what?

Tony tried to excuse himself by saying he had lots of work.

"Don't go away," the author pleaded sarcastically. "I might learn something from you."

So Tony at last straightened up and told the great author, apologetically, of course, that he happened to know people such as were in Mr. D's play and they would never talk or act like the people on the stage did. . . . He begged Mr. D's pardon, he meant no disrespect, but that was his opinion. "I am a very ignorant man," he insisted . . . "and you shouldn't even talk to me." He wanted to like the play, he said, very much, but nobody talks like the people in the play. He said he was an honest man and he felt he should tell the truth. Mr. D shouldn't have asked him. But he did, and now he offered profuse thanks for the two tickets. "Did your wife like the play?" "Oh yes, she liked it terribly much, Mr. D," he said, "but she's ignorant," Tony assured the playwright, "very ignorant, yes sir. She don't know nothing about life," he added apologetically.

The noted playwright's banquet was positively ruined. He felt a terrible letdown. He couldn't think of anything else but of Tony, that dirty, unimportant little janitor, who had made him feel so unimportant and so miserable. Perhaps Tony was right after all, he thought, and the critics were wrong. The janitor's opinion unfortunately coincided with his own before the premiere. He couldn't imitate the late G. B. Shaw, either, who answered to an irate man from the balcony after the final curtain fell on one of his plays: "What can we *two* do against the whole world, my friend?" He knew his play was bad. It reflected only the national hysteria now sweeping the country. When it was all over, his play would be dead as the dodo and he would be forgotten along with it.

His admirers couldn't help noticing his preoccupation. They asked him what was wrong? Had he been hurt by someone? The good people around him insisted that he had no earthly right to be downhearted when he was at the top of his glorious career.

He tried to reassure them that everything was just dandy only . . . he happened to remember a very sad story about the white elephant. Everyone wanted to hear that, so he told them.

"A long, long time ago," he began, "a sorcerer convinced a shrewd and greedy rich man that he could make gold from inferior and cheap materials. The sorcerer would reveal the great secret to him for a tidy sum. Given the money, the sorcerer told him the secret.

"After he secreted the money, he warned him that he must mix all the ingredients in a big bowl for twenty-four hours without a stop. Twenty-four hours without a stop, he insisted. The greedy man eagerly agreed.

" 'While you're mixing the ingredients,' the sorcerer went on, 'don't under any circumstances think of the white elephant. Not even once,' he warned, 'because if you do, the magic will be broken and you wouldn't get any gold.'

"The greedy man agreed emphatically. Not even once would he think of the white elephant, he assured the sorcerer. Why should he? He had absolutely no reason to. But he did. He could think of little else but the white elephant."

That ended the story, but no one understood its implication.

Let me repeat, everyone is born with imagination, but only a few of us bother to use it.

When I saw that picture in the newspaper at first, it conveyed nothing special to me. But I wanted a story, *so I made up one,* my chief product used being imagination.

Try to do something with this story! It's about happiness. It's a tough assignment, I know, but try it anyhow.

A couple, although married for five years, are still *terribly in love.* Now, what can be done about a story with such happy people? If they are so happy, what is there to write about? However, nothing is as black or as rosy as it looks. Let me discover a little crack in their happiness and I'll enlarge it for you. Eventually the crack would widen itself. But since we have no time to wait, let me explore all the possibilities for a healthy conflict.

If it is true that they are still "terribly in love," it will explain that this couple already have arrived at the apogee of human exaltation. They can't exceed it. They're on the top; now, how long can they maintain it? How long can people wear rose-colored glasses? Five years is a long time. How long can a couple worship each other before they step on each other's toes and find out that they are made from clay.

According to the laws of nature, everything must change, and only change itself remains eternal. Thus, the writer can be certain that, for better or for worse, sooner or later a change must occur between these two people. The change will be so infinitesimal at first that it will hardly be discernible. But it will be there, all the same, and will grow and grow until on one fatal day it will burst open. Even the persons involved will be surprised by the explosion.

You might exclaim, "Aren't there any happy marriages any more, which endure a lifetime?" The answer is, "Yes." Yes, there are many. I will discuss them in another chapter. Now we will deal with the disintegration of a happy marriage.

There are countless reasons why marriages break up. Boredom is one. Petty irritations which build up into vast differences of opinion is another. Then there's the perpetual situation of sameness. Never a change for the couple and slowly each becomes invisible to the other. Then there's the "ditto existence," which palls on couples until one becomes the mirror, the other the reflection.

This is the time when the man discovers that there are other women, and the woman finds another man more fascinating than her own husband.

But you wonder, is this the same couple, once so much in love? Of course it is. But even great love, if *nonprogressive*, will fall into a drab routine. The ardour of the kisses will lessen, and the reassurance of the "I love you" will be meaningless.

It's all very simple. Each begins to take the other for granted. Such a stand spells the beginning of the end. It portends the inevitable.

Jealousy, the important auxiliary of writers and playwrights, the forerunner of change, is always handy! In-law troubles are always a good source. It isn't even necessary to step out of the home. Children can be the dynamite to set off the fuse. He finds out that she loves them more than she does him. Another sure sign that a dead end has been reached is when one spouse discovers frigidity in the other.

If you're not on guard, even an innocent hobby can break up a happy marriage! Shall I mention friends interfering with your life? It's not necessary; it's too obvious.

I can go on and on. Any marriage has pitfalls which may lead to disaster. All these reasons I have mentioned really belong to motivation. But since motivation is impossible without imagination, I mentioned them in order for you to sharpen to the nth degree this very important tool, your imagination.

You may wonder how Dostoevski, the great Russian writer, knew so much about crime. Raskolnikov in *Crime and Punishment* kills two women with utmost brutality and cunning. A reader of that realistic and revolting account might imagine that the author knew so much about the subject of murder that he might have committed one himself.

Dostoevski himself never committed a crime. Even if he had heard confessions directly from murderers, no killer could have related his crimes with such clarity as Dostoevski described them.

Even if pronounced sane according to the law, a murderer operates under a terrific emotional strain and many times would be unable to report the crime coherently. In a murderer's mind, under duress, the unimportant incidents are apt to be magnified, whereas the important ones may be minimized.

A killer's mind (although human) must work differently from a normal man's mind. How does a writer decide what is the right psychological emotion and reasoning for a killer? Or for that matter, a saint, a blackmailer, or a philanderer?

How could Émile Zola describe the miners in his *Germinal?* Recount how the blood of these people turned to coal dust? Zola was never a miner. He may have gone down into the bowels of the earth, he may have known miners intimately, but how could he portray their inner life as faithfully as if he had lived it himself.

How could Shakespeare, Molière, Goethe, Gogol, Anatole France, and all the great writers of the world describe characters they never had a chance to know so faithfully that even our own modern psychologists agree that they were startlingly authentic? *Imagination* is the answer. What is imagination? Imagination, to begin with, is thinking.

But it is not ordinary thinking, or not necessarily factual either. One moment it is factual to the nth degree, while the next it is not. Imagination usually enlarges, contracts, or even obliterates objects or ideas altogether.

It may turn the norm upside down. Imagination can be fanciful. Sometimes it creates new out of old, and vice versa.

Imagination creates mental images. It invents without restriction. It creates new, daring concepts.

Imagination is the X-ray eye with which a writer can penetrate a soul, observe birth and death of thoughts or ideas. Imagination helps you see through the eyes of a man or a woman. Imagination is speedier than a supersonic airplane. It's even swifter than the fastest thing in existence, which is light; and light travels 186,000 miles in one second.

Again, imagination is thinking, first of all, and remembering of past events. Every human being is born with it; the same as he is born with eyes, nose, and mouth. There's nothing remarkable about imagination. It is common property.

We notice peculiarities in people only if these are magnified to a degree where the microscopic becomes mammoth.

Lying and gossiping are the sum totals of lack of accomplishment, frustration, or failure. Liars and gossips use imagination for evil purposes. Perhaps they never had a chance or never knew how to use this natural talent in any other way. Why?

In most cases rigid patterns set by our environment or sickness since childhood have caged our imagination. Imagination, like the wings of a bird, atrophies if not used.

No one can become a writer without imagination, just as a legless person cannot become a runner. Imagination is the natural tool of all creative writers. You can be a writer without eyes, legs, arms, but never without imagination.

The question is, why not? What is so impossible about writing without imagination? It is not necessary to be a murderer yourself to understand one, but you must positively have the faculty of imagining yourself to be one.

Why is it so important to imagine a murderer? You can ask the same question about other living characters. You must understand them all. It is imperative that you have the imaginative power to identify yourself with all the people you write about.

No living man ever committed a crime without rationalization. He has been wronged, or is going to be wronged by someone. He is going to be in the future justified for the particular act he is going to commit, however hideous it might be.

A writer must know about his character's rationalization and motivation. It must ring true. You must be able to understand the worst criminal. How can you know whether a reason for committing a crime is right of wrong? *It is simple if you know how to identify yourself with the person you write about.*

The question is, can you burrow yourself into the mental processes of your character.

If you can't do this, your character will seem superficial. The reader will lose interest, because he does not feel what he should and is not reading about a real human being.

If you as a beginner feel that your imagination is not sufficient, there is only one remedy. You must write every available moment.

Remember that a dancer, a musician, a singer studies six to eight hours a day for six or even ten years before he becomes a professional. It is only natural that a writer, who deals with the complexities of the human mind, should need as much if not more practice. You must practice until you feel you have grown muscles on your imagination.

Now, for a last exercise for your imagination. It will be a difficult and a morbid one. If you remain with me for a little while longer, I promise that you'll be more understanding and the wiser at the end.

The last exercise I shall propose now is really simple. Imagine yourself dead. Period. Nothing else. What do you think will happen to the world if you or I suddenly disappear? Would the sun stand still? Would anyone in London, Paris, New York, Moscow, worry and say sobbingly: "So and so lives no more. What will happen to the world?" Do you think that the earth would stop spinning if you or I were to die? Do you think that, except for a few relatives or friends, the world wouldn't continue as before? Do you think that even those who loved you dearly would stop living as before? Nothing will change, my friend, because Nature, the mother of all living, ordered it, and wisely so. In time you'll be so forgotten by all that it will be as if you had never lived.

Then why should you struggle so, to become a writer or anything else, for that matter, if all this is so? This is my answer. You and I want to struggle, even harder, after knowing all this, because, first of all, we love life, and life without conflict is inconceivable. Secondly, we all want to be remembered.

You and I want to force the great *nihil,* the prince of never-never land, to let Clio, the historian of life, carve our names on the imperishable granite tablet of immortality. We want to be remembered to the end of time.

That's why we try to create, everyone according to his own talent, that the world should remember him.

I think that you deserve an immediate reward for your courage and labor in staying with me this far. Imagine facing a pompous jackass now who tries to impress you with his greatness and importance. Look into his eyes and tell him what a glorious corpse he will make, when his time comes. Tell him only this, and nothing more. He'll understand.

To recognize the inevitable gives one a feeling of greatness; also humility and wisdom. To know that no one can escape his fate will make for fuller cooperation in mankind.

# CHAPTER 13

# The Heart of the Matter

### Unity of Opposites

There are little troubles and there are big troubles. For the purpose of a story here is an example of a little trouble:

A couple quarrel and come to the realization that their marriage is washed up and that they had better get a divorce quickly. No great love is lost between them, because, to begin with, their marriage was one of convenience. True, going through the inconvenience of a divorce will be a nuisance, but at least there will not be any heartbreak. I would call such an affair the little trouble.

The big trouble is when a couple can't stand, despise, and hate each other, but still can't get divorced. They are cursed to stay together, perhaps for life. The reason? Perhaps children, whom they both adore. Financial involvement might be another reason. But whatever the reason, this couple can't effect a separation, so I would call it the big trouble.

Stories and plays are written about those people who cannot separate because their lives depend upon one another.

Any one of us can be caught in such a mess where escape seems impossible. The seemingly impossible or dangerous situation will arouse in us a healthy curiosity to find out how an unfortunate person, who has found himself trapped, can extricate himself.

Without such a central situation, no story or play has that magic touch which compels a reader or audience to stay with it until the end.

I would call such an involvement the unity of opposites or the heart of the matter. A story might contain a magnificent character study and be written in a brilliant style; but still, without the central situation, the unbreakable bond which is the heart of all stories, it cannot be a good story or a good play.

*Unity of Opposites* or *Unbreakable Bond* occurs when two people— the protagonist and the antagonist—are held together by certain binding ties that cannot be broken until one or the other is beaten, forced to give in to the other, or destroyed. As we know, the protagonist goes forward in degrees from 80 to 100. He cannot go backward. He is the militant force who cannot change. He might be beaten until there is no other way out but destruction. The antagonist grows from 1 to 100 and goes from pole to pole and changes through the conflict which was started and forced by the militant protagonist.

Let me explain. In *The Silver Cord* by Sidney Howard, the mother is the protagonist. She is determined to separate her son from his wife. Since she, as all protagonists, starts with a fixed idea she starts the conflict at 80. The wife, the antagonist who came with love and leaves with disgust and perhaps with hate grows from 1 to 100.

The question is: What force holds the antagonist in her place? Why does she stay, instead of walking out on the mother who is threatening her? There must be many reasons. The antagonist might feel that the pivotal character is justified in starting that particular conflict. The antagonist perhaps stays to change the pivotal character's mind for their *mutual benefit*.

As the struggle grows in intensity, the antagonist finds that he or she has become more and more involved in the scheme of the pivotal character and now it is almost impossible for him or her to become disentangled.

The antagonist's intention might have been just to save the pivotal character, but after a while this simple intention turns to disappointment, grows into annoyance, then irritation, then anger, and at last, perhaps, revenge.

The *unity of opposites* can be love which progresses from love to hate. The bond, the whip, is always in the pivotal character's hand being held over the head of the antagonist. He has the power to squeeze this invisible chain called the unbreakable bond until the antagonist from sheer necessity starts to struggle to liberate himself from this bondage and save his own life.

If for any reason the antagonist cannot defend himself because of weakness, narrow-mindedness, or religious fanaticism, he cannot be an antagonist. The antagonist *must grow* under the onslaught of the pivotal character.

The antagonist might be motivated to stay and fight because of greed, revenge, indispensability, shame, pride, security, social position, or any of the other human passions that compel a person through hardship to achieve a goal.

[ 118 ]

*Unity of opposites* means to *unite to oppose*. A father can walk out on his wife or even his children if he has no compelling love or passion to be one of the family. A wife, children, business partners can do the same if there is not present a force much stronger than the desire to be free. An antagonist must revolt; he must fight back if he wishes to save his health, wealth, decency, integrity, honor, or very life.

There is nothing difficult about understanding the unity of opposites. Let us look at a few plots we already know.

*A DOLL'S HOUSE*: The bond is simple. Out of sheer love, Nora forged a signature to save her husband's life. She discovers that this act is a deadly sin in the eyes of her husband. Now the struggle is to keep this sin a secret. The bond is broken when the husband discovers what Nora has done.

*KING LEAR*: The king has given all his power to his two older daughters. They in turn, deprive him of the most elementary necessities. He revolts against this bondage. The daughters' shortsightedness and cruelty constitute the "bond" which is broken only when they are killed and Lear himself dies. The bond started as a gesture and ended in tragedy.

The unity of opposites is really the kernel, the heart of all stories. Without it there is no story possible.

My advice is that the moment you have established your premise and your characters, the *next most vital step* is to find the unbreakable bond which is the "unity of opposites."

*MAKING A FIRE*: This short story by Jack London, shows a classic example of an unbreakable bond. A trapper is looking for a short cut and decides to cross a desolate stretch of forest in the deadly temperature of 60 degrees

[ 119 ]

below zero. He feels he can make it. He challenges man's ancient enemy, the cold. Singlehanded, in the middle of the journey, he is overtaken by darkness. He is exhausted beyond belief and on the verge of collapse. He can't go back and he can't go on, but to stay and spend the night in the cold without adequate preparation means certain death. He can save his ebbing life only if he can light a fire. He has matches, all right, and he has firewood on hand, but his stiff, frozen fingers refuse to obey and can't hold a match in their grip and one by one they all fall on the deadly icy snow, thus sealing the man's doom. He collapses after many unsuccessful attempts and freezes to death, as he knew he would if he failed. That broke the bond which existed between the two combatants, the man and the cold. He lost and with his death the bond was broken.

# CHAPTER 14

# Examples of Unity of Opposites

In the following examples the premises necessarily are the author's creation.

Every individual must use his *own logic* and his *own conclusion* in formulating his premise.

The reason: Every person has his own limited or unlimited knowledge of the world around him. There is no sense in telling him to see blue if it is only possible for him to see red and green.

Read over chapter marked *PREMISE.*

A pimp asks more money from a prostitute. Shall she give to him? She has to. She has a sick husband whom she adores. If she refuses the pimp, he might give her secret away.

The pimp is the pivotal character. He starts the conflict and is militant and ruthless. The prostitute is the antagonist, because she is forced to grow to protect her husband. The premise is: Greed leads to its own destruction.

You insult your friend. He is angry and leaves, never to return. But if he had loaned you ten thousand dollars, could he leave so easily, never to return?

The man who got the loan is the pivotal character. He started the conflict by insulting his friend. The friend is the antagonist, as he will be forced to grow from pole to pole because he needs the money. The premise is: Jealousy leads to murder.

Your daughter falls in love with a man who you abhor. Can she leave your home? Of course she can. But will she, if she expected you to put her future husband into business with your backing?

The girl's father is the pivotal character. He started the conflict by hating the girl's fiancé. The girl is the antagonist because she fights back and will be forced to grow. The premise is: Intolerance leads to isolation.

You are in partnership with your father-in-law. You don't like the old man's way of doing business. Can you dissolve this union? We don't see any reason why not. The only trouble is that the old man holds a check you have forged, and he can put you in prison at any time he chooses.

The person who is in partnership with his father-in-law is the pivotal character. He started the conflict by hating the way his father-in-law conducted his business. The father-in-law is the antagonist. The premise is: Disrespect leads to murder.

You are living with your stepfather. You hate him and still insist on staying in his house. Why? You have a horrible suspicion that he killed your father, and you stay to prove it.

The person who is living with the stepfather is the pivotal character, because he starts the conflict and he is ruthless and militant. He started at 90 and will go to 100, suspicion to murder. The antagonist is the stepfather. The premise is: Revenge leads to death.

You divided your fortune between your children, and in return you ask for only one room in their spacious house. Later they become disagreeable, even insulting. Can you pack up and leave them, when you have no means left to support yourself?

The child who started the conflict is the pivotal character. He is ruthless and militant. He started at 90, Greed, and goes to 100, Destruction. The person who divided his fortune is the antagonist, because he grows from 1, Love, to 100, Hate. The premise is: Greed leads to destruction.

A prominent lawyer in a southern town discovers that his son was party to a lynching. Being an honest man, he must turn against his son, but if he does, it will kill his invalid wife.

The lawyer is the pivotal character, because he was forced to start the conflict by forces beyond his control. He must be militant and ruthless, because he wants to save his son. The son is the antagonist. He believes in racial discrimination and fights against his father. The premise is: Belief in equality leads to success.

A man falsely accused of subversive activities discovers that his brother is one of the spies.

The accused man is the pivotal character, because he

[ 123 ]

starts the conflict to free himself. He must be militant.
The brother is the antagonist. The premise is: A strong
sense of honor leads to death.

A woman has an overwhelming ambition for her very
talented son to become another Paganini. She hates her
husband. He is a tyrant, but she cannot leave him because
he provides the high tuition fee for her son.

The woman is the pivotal character, because she is ruthless and militant in her desire to see that her son is given
the opportunity to continue his studies. She starts the conflict by hating her husband. The husband is the antagonist.
The premise is: Ruthless ambition leads to success.

An extremely greedy husband causes his wife to find
love with his business partner. The wife wishes to confess,
but can't tell her husband about her love because he would
destroy his partner.

The greedy husband is the pivotal character, because
he only grows from 90 to 100. He is militant and ruthless
and started the conflict. The wife is the antagonist, because she grows from 1 to 100. The premise is: Greed leads
to suicide.

An ambitious man jilts his mistress in order to marry a
respectable and influential girl whom he loves and who
will be advantageous to his career. The jilted mistress
threatens to expose his love affair with her if he discon-
tinues her support.

The ambitious man is the pivotal character, because
he started the conflict and he is ruthless and militant. He
grows from 90 to 100. The jilted girl is the antagonist,

because she grows from 1 to 100. The premise is: Trickery leads to loss of wealth.

The wife of a racially intolerant husband gives birth to a colored child.

The intolerant husband is the pivotal character, because he started the conflict. He is ruthless and militant. The wife is the antagonist. The premise is: Intolerance leads to insanity.

A scrupulously honest and highly respected banker has a son who steals from the bank.

The banker is the pivotal character, because he started the conflict to save himself and his son from disgrace. He is militant and ruthless. The son is the antagonist. The premise is: Honesty leads to success.

A husband devoted to his children is unable to resist the flattery and attention of other women. The parents cannot walk out on each other because they both feel a responsibility toward their children.

The husband is the pivotal character, because he started the conflict. The wife is the antagonist. The premise is: Promiscuity leads to hate.

A woman with three children lives in a small town and is married to a self-righteous dominating minister whom she has grown to detest. She can't run away because she doesn't want to create a scandal that will ruin the reputation of herself, her husband, and her children. Divorce is definitely against her religious thinking.

The minister is the pivotal character, because he only grows from 90 to 100. He started the conflict. The wife is the antagonist. The premise is: Domination leads to loneliness.

A man is accused of treachery. There is only one man who can vouch for his innocence. But that man hates him more than death itself. Somehow he must make that man clear his name.

The man that is accused of treachery is the pivotal character. He starts the conflict and is ruthless and militant. The man who is his enemy is the antagonist, because he grows from disrespect to respect. The premise is: Fear of disgrace leads to outstanding demonstration of courage.

Joe Smith saved my life in the war. To do this, he knowingly jeopardized his own life. Now he is married and madly in love with his wife, but she is bored with him and is looking for romance. I am determined to save Joe's life in return for my life that he saved. While I am laboring to save his marriage, he accuses me of wanting his wife. I can't tell him the truth without jeopardizing his life.

I am the pivotal character. I start the conflict by endeavoring to save Joe Smith's marriage. I go from 90 to 100. Joe Smith is the antagonist. He grows from distrust to trust, in other words, from 1 to 100. The premise is: Loyalty leads to happiness.

CHAPTER **15**

# *Can an Antagonist Become a Protagonist?*

O N THE following pages are character traits and emotions representing characters. Everyone of them might be a pivotal character or an antagonist. It depends upon what the author wishes to prove.

Let us take an example. Infallibility, for instance; infallibility, as such, is an abnormal mental condition. Such a person is good for the role of a pivotal character. He will grow from 90 to 100. The absolute sureness becomes at the end a maniacal certainty. So his growth will be from mere infallibility to the end of the line—almost madness.

Who can stand up against such a force? Someone who is bound with an unbreakable bond to this man. The person who cannot walk out on him, the person who must see through him to change or break him, or lose his own mind in the bargain. The second person will be the antagonist. The antagonist, who perhaps started out with love, ends up hating or even killing the pivotal character, who is infallible. So the antagonist starts at 1 and arrives at the opposing pole, which is 100.

The infallible person first annoyed the antagonist, who loved him. Then annoyance grew into irritation, irritation into anger and, step by step, the antagonist arrived at the last station, which is hatred or murder.

The infallible person became a pivotal character, because he decided to change his wife into the image of perfection. He started and forced the conflict. The wife, the antagonist, was a passive person to start with, but a constant irritation made her what she became.

Now, we can take the same infallible person and make him the antagonist instead of the pivotal character. How can we accomplish this almost impossible feat?

Very simple. The infallible one is satisfied with his *status quo*. But his wife now becomes the belligerent, impatient one, and starts a crusade against the infallibility of her husband.

If she is militant enough, if she is big enough, if she feels she cannot tolerate abuse and the infallibility of her husband any longer, and if she is desperate enough to decide that she'd rather die than live with such a maniac any longer, this desperation will make a good, substantial pivotal character out of her.

Being a pivotal character, she might start from 80 or 85 and grow in fury and determination which becomes almost maniacal. She is going to prove that her husband is not only not infallible, but naïve as well. Thus, constantly having his shortcomings proven to him, this seemingly immovable, infallible character starts to move toward reason, and, at the end, he himself shall admit that there is no such thing as infallibility. This movement of his carries him from pole to pole which equals 100.

The infallible one becomes a *pivotal character* the moment he decides *to be militant.*

The same infallible one is a mere antagonist *if he is not* militant. He is an antagonist if he is satisfied with his own infallibility and chuckles over those who cannot recognize the wisdom he happens to represent. Now if the "infallible" character is the *protagonist*, it'll be a drama or a tragedy. On the other hand, if the *antagonist* is the pivotal character, the play or story will become a comedy.

Now let's see some of these potential characters for any type of writing.

Is he a chronic blunderer?
Has he any kind of phobia?
Does he insist on being unconventional?
Does he insist on being systematic?
Is he hypersensitive?
Is he inclined to quibble?
Does he insist on being the life of the party?
Is he an inveterate gossip?
Is he overgenerous?
Does he think he is indispensable?
Is he jealous?
Is he an opportunist?
Is he a skeptic?
Is he too wise?
Is he revengeful?
Is he impetuous
Is he ruthlessly ambitious?
Is he greedy?
Is he morbid?
Is he courteous to the extreme?
Is he a drunkard?

Is he imaginative?
Does he daydream?
Is he too immaculate?
Is he a pessimist?
Is he always cheerful?
Is he a hypochondriac?
Is he a perfectionist?
Does he feel neglected?
Did he lose confidence in mankind?
Does he think he is a funny-man?
Does he wish to live dangerously?
Is he romantic?
Is he curious?
Does he believe everything he hears?
Is he a worrier?
Is he ill-tempered?
Is he afraid of life?
Is he forgetful?
Does he constantly correct others?
Is he a social climber?
Is he a fresh-air fiend?
Is he a crook by conviction?
Is he a lady's man?
Does he believe in hunches?
Is he absent-minded?
Is his family superior to others?
Does he believe in advertisements?
Is he smarter than the smartest in the world?
Is he a music lover?
Is he a religious fanatic?
Is he a gambler?
Is he a hero-worshiper?

Does he refuse to grow old?
Does he believe in luck?

Once more, let us see whether the last one, "Is he a believer in luck?" should be the antagonist or a pivotal character? There is plenty of material in him for both roles. A person who believes in luck usually neglects to earn his livelihood with decent labor. If you make him an *antagonist,* he'll be forced, step by step, to the realization that "luck" is elusive. Better knuckle down and do an honest day's work. If you can make him see the error of his ways, *he is an antagonist.*

On the other hand, he can be made a very sinister, ruthless protagonist who with his eternal quest for luck drives people into despair.

The first choice would be really a comedy, the second, a satire, drama, or even outright tragedy.

The same principle governs all the character's traits or emotions we mentioned above.

# CHAPTER 16

# How to Start
# a Story or Play

A STORY is rarely accepted unless it contains a "gimmick." An editor inevitably looks for the "gimmick" in every story he reads. If he is in a good humor, he might explain to you that the "gimmick" is the hook which catches and retains the reader's interest to the end.

The "gimmick" is the something which must catch the readers immediately. A good writer will not create atmosphere first, characters second, and conflict third. He will introduce all these three elements at once.

Some of Hemingway's short stories have the so-called "gimmick" at the beginning, where it belongs, but most of them begin slowly. Many of our well-known writers have the same shortcomings. Some of their stories are breath-taking, and others are dull.

I might as well try to give you my ideas of how to start a good story, novel, or play.

It seems to me that we all have a common interest in trouble. It is something we all experience at one time or other. Therefore it becomes an important matter for discussion.

You could not help but be curious about a couple who had been madly in love, but now hated each other and wanted to get a divorce after years of marriage.

*The correct way to start any story is to begin it at the point where one or more of the characters have arrived at a turning point in their lives.*

A woman has discovered that her husband, a leading citizen in their town, is about to be arrested for the misappropriation of other people's money. The turning point in the situation is when the wife discovers the impending catastrophe.

Here is another example. A prudish man, an outstanding citizen in his community, discovers that the mother of his two children was a call girl before their marriage. The turning point here is the husband's discovery of his wife's past.

Here is still another. While driving his car, the father of three children runs over and kills someone else's child. Upon impulse he runs away. He now can't face his own children. The turning point is when he accidentally kills the child.

A short story differs from a novel, because it deals with one or two incidents in a character's life, while a novel deals with many episodes, one growing out of the other.

While a radio, television, or stage play must start with a *crisis,* or a *turning point,* a short story can start at the preparation of a *turning point* or climax. If an author wants to write a short story about rape, he first introduces the characters. The raping incident will not be at the beginning but at the end of the story. In a play you imply that the raping has already taken place and now write about the characters and the *consequences* they must face.

*A good play starts at the middle of the middle.* The play is the outgrowth, the direct result of what has transpired before. For instance: In *Hamlet,* in the beginning of the play the ghost of the father asks Hamlet to take revenge for his murder. The play itself consists of the revenge, which is the direct result of what has happened before.

In a play we witness the *outcome* of a previous crisis. In other words; a short story is really the preparation, the leading up to a drama. Although a short story consists of only one or two episodes, it still must consist of crisis, climax, and resolution.

*In a play,* the story I told you about the man who misappropriated funds should begin when his wife discovers that he is going to be arrested.

*In a novel,* this same story can begin when the man is forced to take other people's money to save himself from going to jail.

If you want to make this same subject a short story, begin when the man is about ready to tell his wife that the jig is up and he doesn't know what to do.

The story of the man who discovered that his wife was a call girl before their marriage also has all the necessary requisites for a good story or play. It is up to you to choose the medium of writing you find most useful and interesting. *In a drama* this husband suspects that his wife, who really is the epitome of loyalty, has too many male acquaintances. They contact her claiming that they are relatives or former friends of hers. There might be some definite relationships. *In a novel* the author could begin the story where the call girl has decided to turn over a new leaf and get married.

In novel writing you have much more ground to move about in, in getting started. But even in novel writing you must remember that your character has a *past* that she's trying to conceal at any cost.

Remember that all stories and all plays are based on an incident which has *already* occurred.

Here is a premise and a blueprint for a possible conflict that can grow out of it. We illustrate it step by step.

## POSSESSIVE LOVE LEADS TO MURDER

1. Doubt
2. Questioning
3. Suspicion
4. Testing
5. Hurt
6. Realization
7. Disappointment
8. Bitterness
9. Revaluation and failure to adjust
10. Resentment
11. Anger
12. Fury at oneself
13. Fury at object
14. Hate
15. Murder

Granted you know the direction of your story or play, you must know now where and how to start it.

Since the novel is essentially a narration, you can expand, analyze, explain, and philosophize on it, but the play is different in the respect that it is the essence of all that has happened before.

The playwright doesn't have time to contemplate or explain. Everything in a play must come through conflict, including philosophy.

The difference between a novel and a play is comparable to heat and cold. The first expands, the second contracts.

Look at the above chart again. A novel might start with possessive love, which breeds suspicion and revolt against tyranny. This is a good beginning for a novel. To show how possessive love started would be frightfully dull. You can take care of that in one or two sentences later on.

Possessive love usually ends in destruction. We all know that few people can stand possessiveness for too long a time. A good beginning for your novel is at the point where possessiveness becomes *unbearable*.

This is a good point to begin a novel, but not a play. A play is not really life, but the essence of it; therefore, you can't begin the story earlier than the turning point in the life or lives of one or more of the characters.

A play might begin with Suspicion. Suspicion causes activity and conflict. It is a good beginning for a play, because one character already suspects the other and starts to test his loyalty.

Any part of the above chart may be used as a focal point in beginning a *short story*. A short story covers only one or two incidents and then you could complete it by adding a resolution, the natural outgrowth to those incidents. The author should pick which of the many incidents he prefers or which he thinks he can work out the best.

This is how it works. If you start with Doubt from the above chart, the resolution, whether tragedy or reconciliation, will be at the conclusion. The same procedure holds true for any of the other steps with which you begin. As for the other fifteen steps in the above chart, you had better not ignore them. Should you begin your short story with doubt, you still must touch on every step of the above scale before you reach your final resolution.

Again I remind you that you need each of these steps in a condensed form, if you wish to write a good and lasting story.

To the question, where shall we begin writing a story or play, the answer is, the middle of the middle. Here are a few examples.

A woman is about to elope.

A man prepares to murder his wife.

A woman blackmails another woman.

The governor of a state is accused of rape and murder.

A man is about to betray his own country.

A virgin is about to fall into the trap of a philanderer.

A jealous wife believes rumors that her husband has an affair with another woman and kills him.

A business man believes mistakenly that his partner wants to kill him, and kills the partner first.

A man who has been exchanging pictures and letters with a woman from another country proposes marriage and sends for her. When she arrives, he is shocked by the contrast between her pictures and herself in person. He finds out that it is the same woman, only she is twenty years older than the pictures she sent him.

A woman decides to divorce her husband because he lacks the social graces she admires so much in others. She meets and marries a European gentlemen, who has all the social graces, except that he turns out to be a crook.

A young man courts a charming young girl. One day the young girl realizes that the ardent young lover really is in love with her widowed mother.

All these examples are not the beginning but the middle

[ 137 ]

of the stories. A story begun at the very beginning would prove dull reading; a play, a deadly bore in the theater.

Many things have to happen *before* a play opens.

Action stems from the contradiction of elements within us, which naturally results in drama or comedy.

# CHAPTER 17

# The Birth of a Story

LET US suppose that you want to write about a day-dreamer, a person who feels that the world owes him a living, or one who believes that if only he were given the chance to become a lawyer, an inventor, or anything of importance under the sun, he could startle the world in no time at all. He has unlimited confidence in himself, only he doesn't do anything about materializing his dreams. He only talks about them.

A character of this sort makes fabulous story material. Daydreaming is a universal pastime for all of us. We are always ready to blame others for our incompetence and failure.

If this sort of character is worth writing about, how shall we begin to write his story.

No doubt a skillful way to start any story is to engage your central character in conflict. You might ask, why conflict? For the simple reason that a character, any character, even you or I, will in conflict reveal himself in the shortest possible time.

A reader is always eager to read about a saint who became a profligate, or an honest man who became dishonest; yes, it is always exciting to see a daydreamer go through a metamorphosis and become a realist. What power, what invisible force is it that accomplishes this tremendous change?

There isn't any mystery whatsoever involved in this transformation. If you write about an incorrigible day-dreamer, his logical *opposite* would be a realist. Yes, a realist is the force in this case which will transform one thing into another, one character trait into another character trait.

It is advisable to always use opposites facing each other, in all types of writing, if you want to establish conflict from the very beginning.

These opposite characters should be militant, of course. Without militant opposition there will be no conflict. Conflict is life, a static situation is death. In nature there is no static state. From the invisible atom up to the stars, a million light years away, a constant struggle goes on. This struggle has been going on from the beginning of time, and will last through all eternity. Don't think that only man dies. The stars up in the far distance perish the same way, too, as man does down on earth.

To match different kinds of people against one another is called orchestration. This is a vital part of all types of writing. Here are a few examples of how a story, any kind of story, can be begun.

An optimist might be opposed by a pessimist. They are exact opposites, and if both of them are militant, conflict will be inevitable. For the same reason, it is better to pit an honest man against a dishonest man; a spendthrift against a penny pincher; a jolly, happy-go-lucky person against a morbid person. The difference will show up like a white dot on a dark canvas, or a wart on the face. Religious fanatics are best contrasted with militant atheists. A meticulous person should be contrasted with one who is completely disorganized.

If you happen to use two characters of the same kind, you must orchestrate them against one or two individuals who are the opposite of your first two. For example, two immoral people against one or more highly moral people.

Just imagine what would happen if two zealots like a dreamer and a realist were locked in an unbreakable bond, both pitilessly militant, believing 100 per cent that their philosophy of life and approach to life are the only ones that are sound and logical.

There are many different ways to conceive a story. A story might spring from an idea, from a joke, from an incident or from a dream. It can come also from orchestrating two absolutely opposite characters against each other.

If for any reason one of these combatants becomes tolerant of the other's weakness, the story dies stillborn. With a tolerant antagonist you might write a very colorful character study, but never a story where the reader's interest is held to the very end.

A realist thinks of a dreamer as one who commits the blackest of sins; while a dreamer thinks of a realist as a useless fool who doesn't deserve to live.

Now, if you have two characters as opposed to each other as a daydreamer and a realist, you have the foundation of a very good story. But before we can go any further, we should find out why one can't walk out on the other while the conflict is still on.

Let us suppose that the daydreamer and the realist are

married. The man is the dreamer, the woman is the realist.

I shall propose certain things the way I see them, but my example does not necessarily have to be the same as yours. My outlook on life naturally differs from yours, the same as human beings differ from each other. The important thing to remember is that you have two perfectly orchestrated characters who are hell-bent to oppose or even destroy each other if necessary.

I am going to give you my version of an unbreakable bond between these two people. You can formulate your own, if you wish.

The realist, the woman, in their courting days was very much impressed with the man's idealistic outlook on life. It sounded romantic, colorful, and exciting. She was overcome by the eloquent plans this man made for the future. She didn't know then that this man's greatest ability lay only in the planning.

The woman, who was the realist, overlooked at that time the fact that a portion of ice cream can be refreshing, while hundreds of tons of ice cream eaten twenty-four hours a day the rest of her natural life could become deadly.

One mistake leads to another mistake, and another, and another, until one is caught in the trap he shortsightedly built for himself. When he discovers what has happened, he tries desperately to extricate himself.

What could have been the reason that this woman, the realist, could not have seen the man's obvious shortcomings? Let us try to find out those reasons. Let us begin at the beginning. This woman was thirty-one years old, very lonely and very frightened. She worried and wondered if she'd ever meet the right man who'd be willing to marry her. She was a simple girl with a conservative family background and one disastrous love affair behind her. After that sad love episode she became frightened of men. In fact, for awhile she was so lonely and hopeless that she was on the verge of doing something very unrealistic, like committing suicide. But the woman had a little money in the bank and owned a two-family house, left her by her parents. She was employed in a lawyer's office.

When the dreamer came along, she was overwhelmed by the presence of a good-looking male. The dreamer, on the other hand, was very much impressed by her devotion, understanding, and—let us be frank about it—her generous financial assistance to him. He hadn't any qualms about taking money from a woman because he was positive that he was going to become a very great author in a short time, like Hemingway or Dreiser, for instance. Then he could repay her a thousandfold for what she'd done for him.

Yes, the dreamer was an unsuccessful writer. A few of his character sketches were published by small art magazines which gave him a grand feeling of importance but no money whatsoever.

So they were married. At the beginning she needed him and hoped that everything would turn out for the best. The dreamer followed the same line of thought. The woman, being a realist, remained on her job. The daydreamer worked on his great novel, when he wasn't talking about it to his friends. The tragedy was that he talked more than he worked. When the glory of newness wore thin, trouble started.

Who do you think would start the trouble between these two people? I can assure you it wouldn't be the dreamer, because he needed peace and help desperately.

[ 143 ]

The woman, on the other hand, became increasingly impatient with her husband's tardiness, idleness, arrogance, and bragging. The worst blow to his vanity came when she called him a braggart. She called him everything under the sun when she became angry with him, but nothing hurt him as much as being called a braggart. He sulked for weeks at a time, but, since he liked to eat, he usually apologized with great humility and promised to turn over a new leaf.

After five years of this loafing, he began to realize that he had better do something to establish his wife's confidence in him. He couldn't help noticing her restlessness and he was frightened lest she cut out her support, without which he could never finish his life's work, the great American novel. She, on the other hand, hated to throw out this useless bum for the simple reason that she woefully remembered the ache of her terrible loneliness before she had married him. Then, she thought he might still settle down and write the book which would make a fortune. Why not? It had happened to others before. Why shouldn't it happen to them? Such reasoning as this, of course, was born of sheer desperation and not of strict belief in realism.

The unbreakable bond was then forged from the dependence of these two people on one another.

The conflict, the real crisis of their life, began when the dreamer came home one day with a sure-fire proposition. He had the chance of a lifetime, he said, if he could buy himself a half partnership in a small advertising agency. The price is so trifling, laughable, he added, only a paltry ten thousand dollars. The woman's answer was such a vehement no that it started a fight which lasted for weeks.

At last the dreamer packed up his belongings, the little

he had, and appeared ready to leave. It looked as if he meant it this time. No doubt his desperation blinded him to the fact that he really couldn't go anywhere, because without her support he would be lost. In the end she grudgingly gave in to him, fearful of being lonely and lost. The money didn't last long with him. In a few short years everything they had was gone. They were cleaned out.

Luckily she was still working, but the loss of her money made her more insecure and more frightened than ever before. She became sick, mentally and physically. She now was in constant fear that he would really leave her. Now there was nothing to hold him. It was a nightmarish, dreadful existence for her.

She began to cater to his wishes. She became more amiable, more cooperative, and more affectionate to him. The dreamer in a corresponding degree became more hostile and more cruel to her. Confident now that she would never kick him out, he started to play around with other women.

The end? It will depend on what you, the writer, wish to prove.

What kind of premise do you want to formulate? Daydreaming leads to divorce? Or daydreaming leads to murder! He might murder his wife, because she advertises her husband's utter selfishness, cruelty, and dishonesty. She creates scandal after scandal in public, and deliberately goes out of her way to humiliate him. She makes his life so miserable that this worm, the man who never did anything positive in his life, becomes so aroused that in a moment of hysterical fury he kills her.

You might have another premise for this same story: Daydreaming leads to success and happiness. It is possible, you know! The last minute before the last straw breaks the camel's back, something happens. The daydreamer's book is sold and it is a great success.

But if you formulate such an ending, *daydreaming won't be the right premise for your story.* You should change it to: *"Perseverance leads to success and happiness."* A person with dogged determination and absolute faith in his own strength and ability sometimes looks dangerously like a daydreamer, especially if success eludes him for a long time.

The analogy is not exactly good, because while the daydreamer dreams, the persevering man is a "doer" besides being a visionary.

The unity of opposites, the unbreakable bond, makes any story possible. Out of this unity grows your story. The premise is a microscopic form of the story itself.

You might write an outline as I did now and ask yourself what you really want to say. Formulate a premise and start your story at a crisis, which is the turning point in your character's life.

The above story has grown out of orchestration. A daydreamer pitched against a realist, both of them militant and intolerant of each other's beliefs.

A man might be a music lover and meet a young lady who loves music too. The difference between the two is that while the man makes music an obsession, like that of a baseball fan for his team, the girl's appreciation of music is just moderate, normal, and nothing more. At the beginning, their infatuation and their various common interests will effectively obscure the real issue which will grow into such fearful proportions later that serious complications will result.

This story, too, can start from orchestration. Find out why they can't run away from each other in the middle of their struggle—formulate a premise and you are ready to write your story.

Let me repeat: there is rich material for a story if two militant and entirely different types of characters are bound together in an unbreakable union; and as they struggle to break their bonds they will naturally generate rising conflict in the process.

Here are a few examples of perfect orchestration and of the birth of a story.

> Sensitive — Insensitive
> Cheerful — Morbid
> Vulgar   — Spiritual

Take any one character and find his opposite, figure out why they can't separate, although that's the very thing they wish to do desperately, and you have a story.

People are confused and wonder about some person who until a few years ago was a religious fanatic, then mysteriously became a godless atheist. What happened to him?

Or take as another example a sensitive person who becomes vulgar and a disgrace to his family and friends. How can such a thing happen? Or take still another example: a man with a sunny disposition, a born optimist, becomes a pessimist. A loyal person becomes disloyal and treacherous. A frugal person becomes a spendthrift. People have a right to wonder about unbelievable transformations. What causes them? Tell people how such changes take place and they will sit at your feet.

Great stories are those which depict human beings, who grow and change as the stories progress. How to accomplish this tremendous feat? If you wish to see a sensitive person become vulgar, you must orchestrate him against a vulgar person who has the power to push him, to trample upon him till he becomes the opposite of what he was before.

You may have noticed already how I say the same thing over and over again in different ways in order to prove the obvious: Orchestration and unity of opposites are important to all types of stories, plays—especially for radio and television—just as lungs and heart are important to human beings.

You simply must have these elements in what you write.

# CHAPTER 18

# *How to Create Suspense*

SINCE all stories or plays must necessarily be reduced to their essentials, the question is, what is that very vital substance that gets a reader to read on with avid interest or holds a theater audience on the edge of its seats?

Suspense, of course. No doubt every writer wishes to know how this substance can be created. Can anyone do it, or is it the property of a selected few? As far as I know, there's nothing mysterious about suspense.

Let me take one example and show how suspense is created.

When suspense is present in any type of writing, the reader or audience usually becomes excited, emotionally upset, and they're restless until the problem is solved.

What is the greatest emotional stimulus besides love? Sympathetic fear for some one with whom we identify ourselves—a character we sympathize with who is in mortal danger which is not yet resolved. This character is *caught* in a situation where his very existence is endangered. It is a crisis which creates an air of uncertainty, anxiety, and fear for the life of our character in the story or play.

Let me illustrate this with a story. I'll take an example from a previous chapter, "Examples of Unity of Opposites," and try to create suspense.

A pimp asks for more money from a prostitute. Should she give it to him? She'll have to. She has a very sick husband whom she adores. If she refuses the pimp's demand, he threatens to give her secret away, and that would kill her husband.

This is the story in a nutshell. Now I am going to try to create suspense. But first we have to know the story and the people in it. We'll never be interested in these people if I don't let you know something about them first.

I am going to tell you now only of their background. I'll let you know later when the story should start.

The first thing that impresses me is that this woman loves her husband so much that she's willing to do something for him that she hates and abhors with all her heart. On the other hand, the husband also loves his wife so much that if he should find out what she's doing for him, just to keep him alive, he, too, would without hesitation kill himself to save her from this terrible degradation.

And here is the third party, the pimp. Without trying to make this human scavenger blacker than he is, let me put him into the right focus, a position which will show the motivation behind his inhuman act.

We know procurers can't exist without some kind of protection from above. His protecting gangster demands from him more money, because the gangster also has another protecting angel of his own in the person of some crooked police officer, who demands from him more money because his higher-ups also demand more graft from him.

The pimp himself is in a precarious position and he turns the screw on the only one who is in his power, his helpless victim, the prostitute. Now, after knowing all this, we can start to put the pieces together and only then can we create suspense.

How? Let me start at the beginning and ask the question: "What is the most vital emotional factor in this human drama?"

Without any doubt, love. These people love each other. We love to see people in love and being loyal, because somehow we, too, wish that someone would love us and be loyal to us.

The shadow of eternal insecurity is our constant companion. We cannot believe that anyone can really and truly love us for our own sake. There is always a doubt, a doubt which usually grows as time passes by. We want love and loyalty as much as we need air to sustain our lives. The emotion of love, then, between these two people is going to touch us almost like a personal emotion. You see, each one is willing to give his very life for the other. We will be moved, because we always hope that someone will love us so.

Since this emotion becomes so personal, my interest is aroused to the nth degree.

Now we know more or less about their background, but not enough about the people. The writer who writes any kind of story must first know his characters. I have no time just now to sketch in all that. Let it be enough to say that these two people defied convention, family, to be with each other. Their love is that rare phenomenon which endures.

[ 151 ]

All this is not yet the story. You should know still more about them. If a writer wishes to understand a character, I would like him to think of himself. Even a writer has parents, sisters, brothers, relatives, friends, acquaintances, and business people he's associating with. Every character has the same coterie around him in various degrees.

And now the story can start. Chapter One, if it is prose, and Act One, Scene One, if it is a play.

The husband is disgusted with his own inability to earn money and begs his wife to let him die. It will liberate her, he says, from the slavery of earning, slaving for medicine and doctors without any hope whatsoever, in the foreseeable future, that he'll ever be better. In return she reassures him that whatever she's doing is done for her own sake, because if he dies that will be the end of her life too. (Great love never fails to move us.)

After this unbreakable bond is established, in *another scene* the pimp can enter with his demand. He's irreconcilable, too, because he is forced to raise money if he intends to remain in business. He threatens. He'll tell her husband the kind of woman she is.

She knows that the shameful knowledge would kill her husband as surely as poison would, and since she believes *really* that her life is meaningless without him, she will try desperately to make the pimp understand that giving him more money would automatically condemn her own husband to die, because she could not take care of him as she has so far.

The pimp *must be adamant!* After all, he's fighting for his own dirty life too.

The situation, although there is no physical violence in it, will create fear in us for the two lovers, and this fear for their lives will give birth to the necessary suspense which will hold the audience spellbound.

The reader I hope realizes that background or characterization must be simultaneous with the main event—conflict. No time must be lost to sketch in mood or any other material to introduce characters. The characters must be introduced through direct conflict.

Every story is better off, especially a play, if it starts in the middle. It is unnecessary to explain how these two people fell in love, how and why the man became sick, and so forth. All this can be taken care of with a line or two as your conflict progresses.

When the husband begs her to let him die, the author has ample opportunity to tell us about this great love, always through conflict. The husband insists on dying to save the wife and she must insist that if he wishes to die, all right then, they should die together. The man must refuse this solution, because he feels that she has before her a rich and beautiful life, while he'll only be a burden to her.

As you see, there is plenty of conflict here. It is a bitter struggle between the two, because each is ready to give his life for the other.

Conflict alone is not enough to create suspense. *We must care for the people in the conflict.* We wish to see the pimp destroyed or somehow eliminated.

Whatever the woman decides to do, suspense is there for the simple reason that two characters' lives are endangered, and we wish to see them saved.

Even if the characters in a story or play are total strangers to a reader, he'll recognize them through their emotion, because emotion is universal. Fear, anger, jealousy, love, greed, and the rest of the human emotions are the identification mark.

All living persons must have experienced all human emotions, in various degrees, of course, and every one of these emotions leaves behind a distinct scar after the crisis has passed, or even been totally forgotten. But the scar remains and similar experience, even if it is remote to us, like reading or witnessing such incidents, will arouse in us a frenzy of agitated fear, and the old, forgotten scar starts to burn as of old.

If emotion is the touchstone, then it seems child's play to create suspense. Yes, it is easy, but remember that this emotion must be crystal clear. We must recognize it at once for what it is.

If it is fear for the character's own life, let it be fear for that one reason only. If it is jealousy, which is also fear, but a different kind, the reader or audience should know at once that it is fear generated by jealousy.

The moment we recognize what kind of emotion moves the character, and if it is genuine emotion, the contact is made. But how shall one know if the emotion is genuine or not? The characters must act as human beings should, or, to be more specific, as *we would act* in similar circumstances.

Here is another episode from the same chapter as the previous one.

You insult your friend. He is angry and leaves, never to return. But if he lent you ten thousand dollars, can he leave so easily, never to return?

This is only an idea, but in this idea is already inherent the unity of opposites. Let me see if it's true.

A man lent ten thousand dollars to his friend and apparently the so-and-so refused to acknowledge the loan.

Why? But if the man with the money has an I.O.U. in his hand, he doesn't have to worry much. Remember, the man is not in tight financial straits; he just refuses to pay back the loan so trustingly given to him. Is he a scoundrel?

I don't know that yet. I must find out first why a man should sink so low as to refuse to pay back an honest loan to the man who trusted him so much that he gave the money to him without any visible collateral. The friend must have thought him an honorable man and loyal friend who deserved to be helped. What could have happened?

The suspense will come after I've put the story material logically together. Just now I am taking this situation in hand and, since it intrigues me, I try to recreate what could have happened between these two trusted friends.

To repudiate such trust, a man must sink very low indeed, or else he must have a very good reason to do such a thing. Let me create the situation and the reason behind it.

Tom, the man who received the loan, has been married to Elsa for about three years. Peter, the man who loaned the money, is also married. Peter borrowed the money from his friends to give it to Tom, who was about to open a real estate office for himself.

The two men had been friends since early childhood. Tom was a muscular, athletic type, while Peter was not only a scholar, but looked it too. He was a tall six-footer, but skinny as a rod. While they were in elementary school, Tom made it his business to protect Peter against the roughnecks who constantly wanted to exert their superiority over the weak ones. In return Peter helped Tom with his homework. Throughout the years their friendship never wavered. They stayed together, although Tom was

[ 155 ]

stuck in the third class of high school, and being of age, went to work, while Peter, the brilliant student, jumped instead and moved ahead in his studies. They nicknamed him "the genius." Peter wrote learned papers about the Pyramids, Egypt, and related topics, while Tom was kept busy in a brokerage firm.

Years passed by and Peter went abroad to study still more. It took more years before he came back an important person. He became an outstanding authority on Egyptology. He received a professorship in one of our important colleges and he, too, settled down at last. He got married and wrote many learned books on his favorite subject.

The reunion between the two friends was a happy one. Tom was especially happy and had a good time showing off with his distinguished friend whose pictures and articles appeared in many of our slick magazines.

Peter's wife, Joy, was also pleased with her husband's new friends and the two families became inseparable.

It happened at this time that Tom got a very promising proposition. He had a chance to get into a partnership with his old boss, if he could raise ten thousand dollars in cash. He had none and he turned to his best friend Peter for help.

Peter had no money either, but since he saw that Tom's business was a sound one and on the up-grade, with a tremendous possibility for extension, decided to do something about the money. He borrowed from Tom, Dick, and Harry until he had the desired amount.

The business really flourished and to all appearances Tom was now on solid ground as far as his financial future was concerned.

Then something terrible happened. The loan was long

overdue, and Tom seemed to have forgotten all about it. Peter, instead of asking Tom for the money, started to pay back the smaller amounts rather than face the awkward situation of reminding Tom of his obligation.

But one day one of his friends who had loaned him one thousand dollars and who needed his money badly forced Peter to see Tom at last for the loan. Then he got the shock of his life. Tom categorically stated that Peter had never given him a solitary penny, let alone ten thousand dollars.

It sounded like a bad joke to Peter and he tried to laugh it off, but as he pressed Tom further, he realized that Tom was deadly serious.

Peter became desperate and demanded an explanation. Tom, instead of answering Peter's direct questions as to whether or not he intended to pay back the money, congratulated Peter for becoming a father. Peter was astonished; Joy had never said a word to him about having a baby, he said.

"Why don't you ask Elsa, my wife, about the baby you fathered?" and Tom was ready to attack and kill the unsuspecting Peter.

How did this sorry affair start? We must know Elsa, Tom's wife first, if we wish to understand this situation.

Elsa, Tom's wife, was always on a much higher level of intelligence than her husband. She loved to read, while Tom was completely satisfied with the excitement baseball had given him. He was a rabid Giant fan and in the baseball season almost had a nervous breakdown if things didn't go just right with his team.

Elsa, on the other hand, always felt in seventh heaven whenever she had a chance to sit with Peter and Joy and have a good talk on literature or about the East. There wasn't the slightest hint that anything improper could exist between these people, but Tom nevertheless started to feel terribly unimportant as he listened to their high-sounding talk about subjects he never heard of or cared about. Tom slowly became insanely jealous and was convinced that Elsa was Peter's mistress.

Before the story or play could have started, Tom was going around preoccupied with the terrible dilemma about his wife and his best friend. Then, as usually happens before explosions, everything came to a head.

One day as he arrived home at the usual time for dinner —at this point our story or play should start—he saw the house all decorated, flowers all over the place, and Elsa radiantly waiting for him. He looked around suspiciously and asked her why the festive occasion. She demurred. "Later," she said; "after dinner you'll find out." She played with him childishly, happily.

But Tom became madder with every moment and was on the verge of an explosion when at last Elsa told him the wonderful news, that he, Tom, was going to be a father.

Tom needed just this piece of news, but instead of exploding, he sat down quietly, dazed. He never expected anything like this. And just when he was about to recover from the shock, the telephone rang. It was Peter, telling him he must see him immediately on a very urgent matter. It was about the one thousand dollars he wanted to be paid.

"Come, come," he urged Peter almost cheerfully. "I, too, have something important to talk over with you," he assured him.

Elsa didn't know what was going on in her husband's mind, but sensed that something must be terribly wrong.

He refused to talk to her but went into the bedroom and took out his German repeating gun, looked into its barrel to see if it was loaded, and put it into his pocket. Elsa was worried, came silently after Tom, and saw him inspecting the gun. She was horrified, and demanded an explanation.

The suspense starts from here on. This is the very beginning of a story or play. At this point the story is not supposed to be more than three or four minutes old—but behind these happenings stand the whole lives of these people.

The more you know about them the more tense the situation will become. Let me suppose that Elsa married Tom, although culturally on a much higher level than him, because of his loving kindness and self-sacrificing nature, when she needed help. She had a very sick mother at the time, and Tom, without a murmur, carried all the financial burden until her death. Now feeling rejected by the woman he loved so much makes Tom's bitterness almost unbearable.

This, then, is the situation when the play or story opens. The author must be absolutely convinced that Elsa is innocent of all wrongdoing. And if he can make the reader or audience believe this, the tension will grow until it reaches a terrific crescendo.

The trouble between these two people was their difference in temperament, interest in life, or you may wish to call it simply the lack of intelligence in Tom. It is a bad business to marry someone who cannot speak the same language. It breeds misunderstanding.

Let me state again what suspense is: It is fear for someone whom we believe innocent and who is in mortal danger.

And now let us look at another kind of suspense, where

we wish to see that the hateful, the cruel are punished. The object of our hatred is cunning enough to outwit the law and we must be fearful that he shouldn't escape his well-deserved punishment.

The second type of suspense, if it is fulfilled, will give us ample satisfaction, but the first kind, when not revenge but sympathy and love make us fearful, will not only be satisfying to us but will remain as a memorable experience.

There is still another type of suspense: the chase. Some criminal of whom we don't know a thing kills and robs a man about whom we similarly know nothing. No doubt there will be created in this chase a mild kind of interest, the lowest form of suspense.

Through our inherent feeling for justice, we wish to see the criminal apprehended and punished, but the moment this is done, we'll forget the whole mess so completely that, a few minutes later, for the life of us we couldn't remember what it was all about.

Read the great masterpieces in any type of writing and you'll be forced to realize that although they were not written for the sole purpose of creating suspense, they're still the very heart of suspense—for the reason I've said before.

Emotion is the international language of man—but you must know man first to recreate those emotions.

*Suspense is the result and not the origin of conflict.*

# CHAPTER 19

# Why Plays Fail

THERE are are many one-play authors in the theater, although they have written and had dozens of plays produced. These once hopeful exponents of playwriting reached the peak of attainment only once—by accident. These people didn't know *how* the miracle happened in their first production, and feverishly wrote play after play, hoping to recapture the lost magic touch. But to no avail.

As a blind hen, after intermittent, frantic pecking, might accidentally find a seed, a playwright might decide in desperation to write something about an incident he happened to witness, or—better—to have lived. This last resort, frantic decision to find a theme, might make it possible for him to at last achieve something so big that it staggers his imagination. Forgetting the past, right off the bat he'll have lofty ideas: that he is inspired, that Shakespeare had better look to his laurels, that he has arrived atop Parnassus forevermore. Didn't he win a Pulitzer prize, a Critic's Circle Award, for excellent writing? Did he? Yes, he did. His play was good, but he didn't, *still* doesn't, for the life of him, know why. Is it possible?

Indeed it is. The poor success-dazed creature doesn't know that his work achieved excellence for the simple reason that he happened to stumble upon people *he knew intimately*. This close proximity to his characters supplied all the complicated mechanism he needed for his writing. He knew them and knew the *motivations* that made them do what they did.

Yes, he knew the motivation in that case—the prime mover, the yeast of emotion. Without emotion, no adrenalin will pour into the blood-stream. Motivation is the Paul Revere of emotion: "To arms, to arms!" shrieks motivation—and emotion bristles instantly, ready to face the enemy.

Motivation moves silently behind the turmoil. Motivation is the culprit, responsible for all that has happened and shall happen in the future. Motivation is usually obvious when it concerns ourselves; but it is exceedingly difficult to detect this shy, elusive fellow in others.

*Lack of motivation is one of the many reasons why plays fail.*

The matter of writing a play is not a matter of writing an arresting story. A play is much more than a story. A play is not realism either; not even life, but the quintessence of life, condensed, capsuled, into two hours in the theater. To write a play is to look into the mystifying cauldron where our very lives are smoldering in slow fire. To write a play is a serious matter, equivalent to re-creating the highest form of life: human beings.

Does all this mean that we should not attempt to write plays because only a selected few have the genius, the know-how, to write them? Emphatically, no! It all adds up to the inescapable fact that even talented people must prepare themselves with knowledge of the task of writing plays.

Most of the produced plays fail because the majority of these plays are merely badly digested ideas, poured into a mold which *looks* like a play.

*Every character must have a past, a present, and a future* in terms of which three dimensions the character must talk, move, act, grow. The straw men of plays (character-less people) who represent only the present, without any past and future, are utterly unreal people. For the *Present is the child of Yesterday and the father of Tomorrow: Three indivisible elements.*

Playwrights must learn the elements they are working with if they wish to succeed not by accident, but by design. If it was possible to analyze and finally split the atom, I honestly believe it is possible to chart the courses of a good play before it is written.

On the other hand, it is not enough to have good writers. The theater needs, as a necessary counterpart, wise producers—prospectors, so to speak—who have the inside and the knowledge to recognize superior dramatic thought, even though the authors turn up in their offices unknown and shabbily dressed.

The great success of *A Street Car Named Desire* and of *Death of a Salesman* was assured because some of the characters in them not only come to life but give us the impression that we actually know them.

All living characters have a certain universality about them. Human beings, let them be Greek, Roman, German, or American, are basically the same. Only the veneer, their customs, and their ethics make them seem something which they really are not.

Hunger, fear, love, hate, devotion, and all the basic

[ 163 ]

emotions in different degrees are the same all over the world.

A play fails if an author does not create people we readily recognize as ones we know. Living characters put into a slowly rising conflict where they are forced to reveal their innermost nature usually give, not only an unforgettable evening in the theater but success and lasting fame for the dramatist.

# CHAPTER 20

# *Happy Marriage*

THE FOUNDATION of all writing is human relationships. What is more human than to get married? Marriage becomes important only if it teaches us how to go about being happy—otherwise it will become the breeding ground of abuse and hatred.

People are forever scheming, fighting, robbing, even killing each other for a nonexistent something called security, so it is not at all strange that they should do the same for the apogee of most dreams—a happy marriage. It is generally believed that if someone achieves a marriage in which there is a possibility of success, this state can be tucked away, hidden, kept intact, as you would secrete a precious stone.

People cannot seem to grasp the idea that happiness is as elusive as a stray summer breeze which ruffles your well-groomed hair on a stifling hot summer day—you start to sigh with relief when that cool, refreshing wind is already becoming a memory.

Happiness, although a state of mind, is subject, like everything else, to the inexorable necessity of change. According to science, the universe is not the same for any two successive seconds; it changes, grows older, and minute by minute ticks itself into eternity. There are many Fridays, but never two the same.

Happiness also goes through a metamorphosis. What the two people involved do with it is up to them. It is the greatest folly to think that happiness, once secured, will remain constant for the rest of our days.

Ask any mother what infinite care goes into the bringing up of a child. But all that eagerness, patience, foresight, tenderness, and love are nothing beside the care with which you have to nurse along a happy marriage, which will never grow up.

You cannot ever say, as a mother does, "Now he knows better, I can relax." If you do, happiness will die of neglect. Happiness is precious. A wrong gesture, a misunderstood look, a missing smile, can do irreparable damage.

Nothing in nature is static; a static state is nonexistent. Not even death is static, because the moment a body stops functioning, a transformation into a different shape and content begins. Being static, like being secure, is only a concept. Happiness, on the other hand, is real, but short-lived.

Now, if we are aware that happiness is quite a fluid thing, we must be prepared to take care of it if our good fortune brings us face to face with it. What qualifications are needed to handle and care for happiness properly? Is it in the province of us all to have it, to keep it, and live with it?

The answer is—*yes*.

*Q:* Now that I know what a slippery thing happiness is, would you be so good as to tell me, if you can, what this blessed state looks like, how it can be recognized, and where it can be found? But first tell me, were you ever happy?

*A:* I have always been so feverishly busy that at this moment I can only say, "I don't know."

*Q:* Then you really don't know whether you were happy?

*A:* Your question can't be answered as easily as that, my friend. We must find out first what the chemical make-up of happiness is; and after we know something about it, we shall try to apply it to a particular state, as, let us say, happiness in marriage.

*Q:* I don't think you'll be competent to answer this question for me, since you admit you don't know whether you were ever happy.

*A:* You are here to check up on me.

*Q:* But, if you don't know what happiness is. . . . Ah, I see a gleam in your eyes and I can almost hear you asking, "Do *you* know?" My answer is the same as yours: "I don't know, either." This is the very thing I want to find out for myself.

*A:* Then let us explore all the possibilities together. I find that even those who claim that they are happy, or were happy, have their own definitions for happiness, so divergent that I have to remind myself that they are talking about the same subject as I am.

*Q:* Since we are looking for truth, we may as well first find out how we can recognize this so-called happiness.

*A:* I was really startled before, when I realized the importance of your question. I said I had had no time to consider whether I was happy. It is true. All my life I have been working—reading and writing. It was a full life. But who made me do those things? Let me see. Work was, and is, a necessity, but who forced me to

[ 167 ]

read whole libraries? Who threatened to kill me if I didn't write during every spare moment of my waking life? No one. Then why did I do it? A compulsion or drive from inside, I suppose. I was not interested in money. I did it for my own satisfaction. It must have been an agreeable sensation to write if I persisted through a whole lifetime.

*Q:* That's the point. Don't you think you were writing because that made you happy?

*A:* Perhaps, but I still don't know what happiness is. Sometimes writing was even more than a pleasurable sensation. Often it was a revelation even to myself, when I captured some difficult phrase with ease. Let me see what the dictionary says about happiness: "Happy—Lucky, fortunate, successful; (2) Being in the enjoyment of pleasurable sensations from the possession of good; enjoying pleasure from the gratification of appetites or desires." According to this definition, happiness is not something made out of a big piece of cloth. Rather, it seems life serves it in small doses to us.

*Q:* Have you any objections?

*A:* It doesn't matter whether I object or not. But what are the component parts of happiness? At this moment, I am a bit taken aback to read that . . . "enjoying pleasure from the gratification of appetites . . ." is what Webster considers being happy. On second thought, why not? Let us suppose that someone has had an ulcer or cancer or diabetes or any of a dozen other diseases, and food which he would have liked to eat was poison for his constitution. At last he's cured. Now he can eat! Heavens, what a pleasure! What a joy! Yes, yes, I can imagine that food for the gourmet or for the starving can give immense pleasure, and, as such, it is one type of happiness—an annex, so to speak to the main building. Fulfillment of desire, ditto. Kissing someone can be happiness if we consider it a rare privilege to kiss that person. Dancing to music, wearing a garment we especially love—these are also forms of happiness. A good talk with friends can make one happy. Drinking a glass of cold beer, having a good night's sleep, and. . . .

Q: Suddenly you seem sour and very unhappy May I ask why?

A: Not unhappy, just a bit disappointed. I thought happiness was much more than eating a good piece of steak.

Q: What did you think happiness was?

A: I really don't know, but I thought it much bigger than a good night's sleep, or a healthy movement of the bowels.

Q: Did the dictionary say anything about what you've just said?

A: No. I only presume that if a meal can make one happy, anything which gives pleasure—whatever it is—is happiness. By the way, according to this, I must have been the happiest man in the world. Writing has given me many sad, many disappointing days, weeks, and months, but nevertheless I have basked in the life-giving joy of accomplishing something I particularly loved.

Q: Is that happiness, then?

A: It sounds moronic, perhaps, but I can't believe that all this is happiness, the dictionary notwithstanding.

Q: That's how I feel about it. Somehow it doesn't sound right. Happiness must be something more substantial, something more profound. Do you agree?

A: Let me see what else the dictionary has to say. Now, " (3) Prosperous; having secured possession of good." It seems being prosperous also makes one happy. But let us not jump to conclusions. " (4) Supplying pleasure; furnishing enjoyment; (5) Dexterous: ready; able; apt; (6) Harmonious; living in accord; enjoying the pleasure of friendship." No, my friend, I don't like all this. There must be more to this than laughter, hilarity, satisfaction, pleasure, joy, luck, success, delight, blissfulness, and prosperity, as well as many others.

*Q:* If not all these, what then?

*A:* All these are good, desirable things that men fight and even kill for, but are they happiness? They must be part of it, but not the whole.

*Q:* Are you sure?

*A:* Not yet. I am searching; I am on the lookout to find the meaning of this rare state of mind.

*Q:* Why do you say, "rare"?

*A:* It must be something which cannot occur every hour or day. Happiness must be the zenith, the height of man's strivings.

*Q:* How do you know?

*A:* I don't know, I am merely talking out loud. If happiness were commonplace, we would not sacrifice our health, our fortune, and many times our soul, for it.

*Q:* Don't we do the same thing for a pair of shoes when we are in dire need of them?

*A:* Yes, we do, but they are a necessity. Happiness must be the epitome of all pleasure, heaven on earth. But I've collected a few interesting opinions about marital happiness. Since we are all striving toward the same goal, the secret of real happiness, we may *find it* in marriage. Who knows? A love marriage, of course. I think I shall dig up those answers I collected years ago and we will scrutinize them together. . . . Here they are. The ques-

[ 170 ]

tion I asked my pupils was: "What qualities do you consider necessary to complete happiness in marriage?" The following is from a man who is sublimely happy with his wife. I don't know whether his wife enjoys the same blessed state.

1. Unprejudiced
2. Good companion
3 Honest
4. Good-natured, amiable
5. Good-looking
6. Neat
7. Good sense of humor
8. Good mother
9. Physical and mental strength.

You will notice that he never mentioned *sex or love.* The next one is a married woman, who worships her husband.

1. Love
2. Compromise
3. Foresightedness
4. Temperance
5. Imagination
6. Sacrifice

This woman appears to be really unselfish; giving without thinking how much she is getting in return. In reality she is getting the greatest security. The following is from a man who was divorced, fell in love and married again, then divorced his second wife.

1. Same political belief
2. Great tenderness
3. Similar background
4. Attractive

5. Should have career
6. Quick mind

The following is from a woman who was married twice. First husband died. Second one divorced.

1. Sex harmony
2. Mutual understanding
3. Economic stability
4. Ability to adapt to new situations

The next is from a very intelligent lady.

1. Kind
2. Good mind
3. Good-looking
4. Pride in appearance
5. Pride in knowledge
6. Belief in his faithfulness
7. Confidence in financial security
8. Belief in his capacity to grow
9. Attracted by differences in character, locality and habits.

As I see it, every one has different conceptions of happiness. Apparently no one can make a blueprint for this ethereal thing, because everyone is trying to fashion it, model it, and formulate it to suit their individual taste and needs.

When one talks about rest, we know what rest means. Laughter signifies humor or joy; sadness means bad news, sickness, or the loss of something dear; the treachery of a friend. We more or less agree on what constitutes friendship. Only happiness stands alone, aloof.

What do we really want, not only from marriage, but from life? Happiness, of course. Let me ask again, what is happiness? It must take its meaning from something we already know, something we can visualize, something we dream of, yearn for, but apparently can never get.

In the final analysis, it seems to me, *we all consider happiness, if we come into possession of it, something we needed most in our WHOLE LIFE.*

If a man missed kindness in a previous marriage, then for him the first requisite in a woman will be kindness. The same goes for tenderness, which is something else again. If some one missed satisfactory sex relations, necessarily sex relationship will take first place in that person's life.

If poverty has dogged a man all his life, he may become a miser, and the accumulation of money will be the prime interest in his life.

*Q:* Something very disturbing has occurred to me. I think I can go along with your interpretation of happiness as the possession of what we need most in our life, whether it is a clean bed, good food, or women. We do everything in our power to secure the precious something, but who can guarantee that we will not lose it the next instant?

*A:* No one.

*Q:* Then happiness is a short-lived state of mind. Webster says good food, good this or that, can create the sensation of happiness. I am afraid that I go along with him. What about you?

*A:* I'll go along with him, too.

*Q:* What have we found out then, that we hadn't known before?

*A:* For myself, I now know that I was not only happy more often than I could ever have imagined, but that my happiness was enduring, and, if possible, deepened with time, because I was doing what I consider the greatest joy in life—*writing.*

[ 173 ]

*Q:* Yes, but how about others?

*A:* Everyone must crystallize for himself what he has missed in life, or what particular thing would make him happier. When this person at last achieves his hard-earned goal, he knows he has in his possession what he always wanted. And when he reaches this exquisite moment of fulfillment, he is at last face to face with happiness.

*Q:* Is that enough for a lifetime or striving?

*A:* No. Fortunately or unfortunately, the moment our goal is reached, we usually go sour on it. I don't think anyone can live just to achieve a single goal. There must be a series of goals leading us on and on. Hold onto a precious thing too long, and it loses its value (the best steak, too much song, too many women, and too much liquor can become satiating).

Some people are very well aware of what they want and fight hard to get it. Then, when their desire is fulfilled, not only disappointment and unhappiness but stark tragedy stares them in the face, for the simple reason that *they refuse to understand that they must go on to ANOTHER GOAL.*

They must relinquish that one blessed moment of fulfillment because what they cling to now is the disintegrating corpse of yesterday.

Let me suppose you marry your beloved, and your relationship to each other is idyllic, still this love cannot last forever. This great loves goes through a transformation every minute, and of necessity becomes something else, in a *week, perhaps, or in a month, or in a year.* One thing you can be sure of: it will change. It must, because that is the eternal law of nature.

The man who said the first thing he wanted from a

woman was political understanding, had wanted sex, first, in his marriage, because there was a political difference between them that spoiled their sex life. Now he demands political harmony first, of his second marriage, to insure his sex harmony.

What am I supposed to get out of this discussion? I hope to remember that happiness is a composite, and not one single thing or one single desire. Happiness, like everything else, goes through eternal transformations. What was happiness today may be unhappiness tomorrow.

Q: You have not yet answered my original question. How should one choose a mate for marriage?

A: The answer was inherent in the previous statement. Happiness results when we come into possession of something we needed most in all our life. If you've never missed or desired anything, you will never be happy either.

The first indication of what we need most in marriage is found when we fervently and consistently admire some trait or conduct or physical attribute or mental accomplishment in *another person*.

This admiration is usually an indication of what we haven't got, or rather of what we would like to be. A mate with his quality, it seems, is the perfect compliment to our character. It must be; otherwise, we would not admire it.

Let me emphasize once more: The constant setting of new goals is of primary importance to everyone in order to insure perpetual happiness. Mankind must find new goals, new premises to fulfill. We must go further, ever further, if we wish to live in peace and contentment. Nature, the mother, never for a moment stops perfecting her creations.

In a human body, millions of cells die daily and mil-

[ 175 ]

lions of new vigorous cells take the place of the old. Can one say to the cells as Joshua did in biblical times to the sun: "Stop. Don't move!"? Obviously not. Whether we like it or not, cells die and new ones are born every minute until the time comes when no new change is possible. The cycle of life is finished. It is the end. It is the end for an insect, a man, our earth, or the universe; it makes no difference. When change is stopped, life stops; then it starts all over again.

Yes, this fundamental law works in marriage as in friendship, and for everything living. Anyone who believes in one *single goal* is courting destruction and death before his time.

# CHAPTER 21

## *The Man Who Wants to Commit Suicide*

Here is an experiment in writing. It is a short sketch. There is nothing greater, nothing worthier to live for—than life. Of course this is a one-man opinion. There are people—a young man is especially in my mind just now—who feel that being dead would be preferable to being alive. To write about a state of mind like that is quite intriguing, to say the least. I am going to try to recapture the man's mental outlook as his tormented mind sees it.

His mother will be the pivotal character and he is the antagonist. The mother starts with confusion and goes to bitter determination. The young man starts with anger and despair and grows to understanding.

As usual the pivotal character carries the premise. The mother in her desperation forces the issue to the breaking point and saves her son.

It seems "Filial love conquers death" tells the story. As you remember, every premise is a thumbnail synopsis of a story or play.

After reading the following scene, find the unity of opposites, orchestration, point of attack, and the rest. If you can't find any of the important parts, it won't be your fault—perhaps they're not even there.

(A room in the Smith household in a suburb of Yew York. A garden around the one-family house can be seen thorugh the windows.

The room is simple, not expensive, but cozy and colorful.

Time: 6 P.M. It is late May. At rise table is set for two. Mrs. Smith comes in with plates. As she puts them on the table, one plate slips out of her hand onto a chair. It breaks and some of the pieces fall on the floor. She stops, looks at broken plate, then sits down dazedly and stares at it. The telephone rings. She pays no a t t e n t i o n , just stares. Phone keeps on ringing.

Finally she comes out of her lethargy and answers it.)

MRS. SMITH: (At phone.) Hello? No. Paul isn't home yet. Who is it? . . . Just a minute . . . let me think. Oh . . . he'll be home any minute. I'm sorry . . . I wasn't thinking . . . I . . . who is this please? Who? Susan . . . Willowby? Do you want him to . . . oh, you'll call back? All right. I'll tell him. (Hangs up phone. Sits and stares ahead of

her. *Noise from outside. She starts. Gets up and begins picking up broken plates.*)
(*The sound of door slamming is heard.*)

PAUL: (*Enters. He is a tall, pale, slim young man.*) Hello. (*He's going out into the kitchen without a stop.*)

MRS. SMITH: Paul . . .

PAUL: Yes?

MRS. SMITH: Didn't you forget something?

PAUL: Did I?

MRS. SMITH: You've never forgotten to kiss me before.

PAUL: Oh. I'm sorry. (*Comes back, kisses his mother perfunctorily, and is ready to leave again.*)

MRS. SMITH: You told me to remind you of the Ursula and Cardiff seeds.

PAUL: I did? Thank you, Mama. (*He leaves the room.*)

MRS. SMITH: (*Goes to door.*) Paul, may I ask you something?

PAUL: Just a minute. (*Splashing of water is heard. Paul enters, drying his hands.*) Yes?

MRS. SMITH: (*Has been crying but now dries her tears.*)

PAUL: What is it?

MRS. SMITH: Something's in my eye.

PAUL: What was it you wanted to ask me?

MRS. SMITH: (*Looks at her son for a moment, but instead of talking walks out of the room.*)

PAUL: (*Goes to door.*) What is it? Please, Mama, what have I done?

[ 179 ]

MRS. SMITH: (*Comes back with two glasses of tomato juice.*) Nothing.

PAUL: If you want to play hide and seek, it's okay with me. Supper ready? I am hungry.

MRS. SMITH: (*As she's leaving room again.*) Wallace called.

PAUL: What did he want?

MRS. SMITH: We're to be at his office tomorrow morning at ten. The store's been sold, he said. There's five thousand dollars left from your father's estate.

PAUL: I am not going. It's your money. You go.

MRS. SMITH: You have to sign the papers too. You're his son.

PAUL: I'm *your* son, not his.

MRS. SMITH: Oh, Paul! Why can't you forget? He's been dead two months. . . .

PAUL: (*With suppressed venom.*) He's still here! I still see him sitting there, his hairy hands on the dining-room table . . . looking at me with those deadly cobra eyes . . .

MRS. SMITH: You must forget, son, you must!

PAUL: (*Laughs bitterly.*) Tell the ventricles of my heart not to contract at the sound of his name!

MRS. SMITH: I'm sorry, Paul. I wouldn't have bothered you, but Wallace said . . .

PAUL: (*Stands up.*) Thanks for supper.

MRS. SMITH: But you haven't eaten yet . . .

PAUL: You mentioned his name, didn't you? That was enough.

[ 180 ]

MRS. SMITH: You're being unfair. Your father wasn't any worse than most old-fashioned Germans who thought . . .

PAUL: Let's drop the subject. (*Pause.*) I stayed home these past years because I couldn't bear to leave you alone with him. And now you're defending him! That's really interesting!

MRS. SMITH: He was my husband.

PAUL: (*With bitter irony.*) Ha! The slave defends the tyrant, who condemned her to life imprisonment!

MRS. SMITH: No one forced me to stay with him.

PAUL: Anyone who accepts tyranny without rebelling deserves his fate.

MRS. SMITH: Don't throw those high-sounding words at me. You know so much, then tell me, where could I have gone? I came from an orphan asylum. No relatives . . . no friends . . .

PAUL: Anything would have been better . . . a cook . . . a housekeeper . . . even a streetwalker . . .

MRS. SMITH: Paul! Please . . .

PAUL: Then stop defending him! He was a Hitler, and you know it. Hitler! He not only beat me . . . I might be able to forget that . . . but you . . .

MRS. SMITH: Only once . . . I paid out a large bill twice!

PAUL: You must have paid out many bills twice!

MRS. SMITH: You shouldn't have stayed home for me, son. (*Silence.*) A girl called you. Susan Willowby, she said. Who is she?

PAUL: Just a waitress in the place I worked last week. (*Goes to window.*) Where did you put the seeds?

MRS. SMITH: (*Eagerly.*) In the hall closet. Are you going to start your crossing?

PAUL: Maybe.

MRS. SMITH: It would be wonderful. . . . Summer-long tulips. Nobody ever thought of crossing the Ursula and Cardiff before . . .

PAUL: (*Snaps.*) All right!

MRS. SMITH: You used to enjoy your flowers so . . . you should . . .

PAUL: I said all right! (*Silence.*)

MRS. SMITH: (*Goes to kitchen and returns with food. Sets it on table and they start to eat.*) Why didn't you go to Tom's housewarming last night?

PAUL: Very simple. I didn't feel like it.

MRS. SMITH: They're playing chess at George's house to-night, aren't they?

PAUL: Are they?

MRS. SMITH: Oh, Paul, did you forget, George asked you over? (*Silence.*) You never see your friends anymore.

PAUL: They're married.

MRS. SMITH: They still like you.

PAUL: I'm a bachelor. I don't belong.

MRS. SMITH: That's foolish.

PAUL: I'm sick and tired of their war stories. They make me feel like a yellow rat.

MRS. SMITH: You did your part. Everybody knows that.

PAUL: Yeah! I was selling bonds while they were dying.

[ 182 ]

MRS. SMITH: You couldn't help it if your heart . . .

PAUL: Thanks to my dear father . . .

MRS. SMITH: You're unfair. People are born with weak hearts sometimes and . . .

PAUL: According to many specialists mine is a fibrosis; a heart block; origin, nerves; cause, father. The tomato juice is very good.

MRS. SMITH: He's gone. Can't you stop hating him?

PAUL: Evil lives on . . . and he was evil, Mama.

MRS. SMITH: Hatred is a sickness, Paul.

PAUL: Yes, I know . . . psychosomatic. It's all in your mind. . . . True enough . . . so tell the world to stop making so much noise. We want to be healthy.

MRS. SMITH: You didn't sleep last night. I heard you walking.

PAUL: And you worry too much.

MRS. SMITH: If you were a mother, you'd understand. We worry about our children when they're small . . . and a hundred times more when they're grown up.

PAUL: Thank goodness I'm not a mother.

MRS. SMITH: (*Exists and comes back with salad bowl.*) I was thinking of Georgiana today.

PAUL: (*Surprised.*) Georgiana?! Why?

MRS. SMITH: She must have given you a very bad shock.

PAUL: I've forgotten all about her.

MRS. SMITH: Have you? I'm glad. Two years is a long time. Time enough to forget.

[ 183 ]

PAUL: What made you think of her today?

MRS. SMITH: I don't know. . . . You . . . you've been so gloomy lately . . . I was trying to figure out why you're so irritated . . . and suddenly I realized that this change started when you broke off with Georgiana.

PAUL: *I* broke off?

MRS. SMITH: What's the difference who broke off? In time you just have to forget and . . .

PAUL: Just like that, hey? When a girl walks out on you two weeks before your wedding . . . you just say to yourself, "Brother, you must be pretty lousy." And then forget all about it!

MRS. SMITH: Don't talk like that!

PAUL: No sane girl would do that without a *very good reason.*

MRS. SMITH: You're a wonderful boy . . . good-looking . . . brilliant . . .

PAUL: Perfect—except for a bum heart and crippled . . .

MRS. SMITH: Crippled?! Where? How? What are you talking about?

PAUL: (*Laughs bitterly.*) You don't even know. My shoulders . . . lopsided. Look.

MRS. SMITH: (*Too astonished to answer at first.*) You . . . (*Laughs.*) Lopsided!? That's news to me. What else?

PAUL: When I meet strangers I stutter like a fool.

MRS. SMITH: And that's a reason to hide from the world?

PAUL: I have too many reasons. Remember what Papa always said, "A son of Germany should be 'Vollkommen!' Perfect!"

MRS. SMITH: You hated him so much, why should you care what he said? No . . . you can't be serious. You simply can't!

PAUL: They don't want me! I told you. I tried . . . I tried!

MRS. SMITH: (*Outraged.*) I don't believe it. Good Lord . . . the whole world is open for you. Women are desperately looking for a good man . . . like you . . . and you think that every girl is like that Georgiana. There are rotten people and there are good people. (*Gets up from table and walks about in bewilderment.*) No! No! Not my son . . . He used to be brilliant. People used to come to you for advice.

PAUL: Fools.

MRS. SMITH: A human life should depend upon such trivial misunderstanding?

PAUL: Apparently. Sit down and finish.

MRS. SMITH: (*Sits down.*) There are movie stars with large ears, large noses . . . and women still love them. What's happened to your wonderful intellect?

PAUL: Intellect . . . and logic are like a telescope. You can see through it only when you look at others . . . from a distance.

MRS. SMITH: You must go to a doctor.

PAUL: You mean a psychiatrist? What for? So he can make me believe I'm an Adonis? He'd have to make me blind and moronic first.

MRS. SMITH: No . . . you'd rather take an overdose of sleeping pills . . .

PAUL: (*Flares up.*) That was an accident!

MRS. SMITH: Was it?

PAUL: I had to sleep . . . I was going crazy with those income taxes . . . I had to sleep . . . (*Pushes away his plate and stands up.*) Why did you have to bring it up now?

MRS. SMITH: I'm sorry. Finish your supper. It's just . . . I want to see you married. I want to know you'll have somebody to take care of you when I . . .

PAUL: I went after June, Marion . . . Helen. . . . They married my friends. Now leave me alone.

MRS. SMITH: Sit down, Paul, please. (*Paul sits and pushes food around his plate without appetite. Pause.*) I just don't understand. You say women don't care for you . . . but I've always seen you act superior to them as if you . . .

PAUL: A common trick of all miserable creatures like myself. They don't notice me. In return, I too refuse to notice them.

MRS. SMITH: You must have humility.

PAUL: Shall I go down on my knees?

MRS. SMITH: Why not? If it's necessary.

PAUL: I will not! When I know at the end . . .

MRS. SMITH: You don't know what will happen at the end.

PAUL: I know. It happened.

MRS. SMITH: What about the girl who called? Miss Willowby? Is she after you?

PAUL: Now why would she be after me? She wants help with her income tax.

MRS. SMITH: Income tax? It's the middle of May.

PAUL: She's stupid.

MRS. SMITH: You're stupid. Can't you tell she's after you?

PAUL: Anyway, I don't trust her.

MRS. SMITH: Do you trust any women?

PAUL: (*Bitterly.*) Why should I? (*Goes to window and looks out.*)

MRS. SMITH: The tulips are coming out beautifully. (*Silence.*) You were so happy with your flowers. Crossing them . . . creating new varieties. You promised to make our name famous. Remember, son?

PAUL: You shouldn't have brought up that . . . Georgiana. She's been dead and buried for . . .

MRS. SMITH: So is your father dead and buried and still you can't forget him. Everything started with that woman. She . . .

PAUL: Nonsense. The straw that broke the camel's back. . . . How many thousands of straws must be there first before. . . . Oh, for God's sake, what started you on this. . . . Can't you leave me alone? Are you taking up where Father left off?

MRS. SMITH: Don't say that! I'm a mother . . .

PAUL: Merciful God, how many crimes are committed in that name?

MRS. SMITH: We only want to help . . .

PAUL: But I don't need your help. (*Shouts.*) I am beyond help . . . I mean . . . help of your kind. You've torn open old wounds. . . . They hurt . . . can't you understand that? They hurt. The past is dead . . . do you hear? Dead, dead!!!

MRS. SMITH: One minute the past never dies and the next . . .

PAUL: I can't make you understand . . .

[ 187 ]

MRS. SMITH: All right. All right. (*Silence.*) Listen . . . I have an idea. Let me give a party for you, Paul. I'll invite some nice girls. It'll be a small party because of Papa . . .

PAUL: Just what I need! A man thirty years old has to have his mother. . . . My God! (*Laughs harshly.*) Trying to make me appear more ridiculous than I am already?

MRS. SMITH: I'm just trying to help you . . .

PAUL: It's too late for that. Perhaps . . . I don't know . . . maybe if I could have gone out with the boys when I was young . . . had fun like they did. But no . . . I had to spend my life in that rotten grocery store with that dictator on my neck!

MRS. SMITH: To think that one woman could do such damage.

PAUL: Forget it, Mama . . . please!

MRS. SMITH: You know what I would like to do, Paul?

PAUL: Yes. . . . Tell the whole world you have the most wonderful son . . .

MRS. SMITH: Yes . . . yes, I would.

PAUL: That's enough for today, Mama.

MRS. SMITH: Anything is better than giving up hope . . .

PAUL: I said, that's enough . . .

MRS. SMITH: Can't you try once more . . . once more . . . for my sake? You're all I have.

PAUL: I'm tired . . . tired of trying . . . tired of everything. Tired of you! (*He's going out.*)

MRS. SMITH: Paul . . . for my sake . . . before we die! .

PAUL: (*Shocked, whirls back.*) What did you say?

MRS. SMITH: Don't you think I know? Do you think I'll let you go alone?

PAUL: What the hell are you talking about?

MRS. SMITH: (*Goes to table, opens drawer, and takes out a revolver. Puts it on table.*) This . . . I found it in your bureau, under your shirts.

PAUL: Goddamn it, you've no right to . . .

MRS. SMITH: I don't want to stop you, Paul. It's all right. If you're such a coward . . . you shouldn't live.

PAUL: Why don't you leave my things alone?

MRS. SMITH: Go ahead. (*Grabs gun and tries to push it in his hand.*) Kill yourself. But do it quickly!

PAUL: (*Takes gun.*) I'll do it when I'm ready . . .

MRS. SMITH: You're ready now. . . . With the sleeping pills you failed. Try now with the gun. . . . Only . . . take me with you. . . . (*Breaks down and sobs.*) Take me with you!

PAUL: Mama! (*Throws gun on floor. Goes to her and takes her in his arms.*) My poor darling. What have I done to you?

MRS. SMITH: Will you try, son, once more? For me? Will you?

## BLACK OUT

The blending of many large and small incidents make a character come to life. Paul's displeasure is understandable from his point of view, but to his mother his attitude seems like sheer cowardice. In trying to save him, she is actually fighting for her own life.

[ 189 ]

Paul's hopelessness is a sure sign that he is desperate enough to throw away his life.

Great emotions that clash reveal people as nothing else will.

# CHAPTER 22

# Writing for Television

Anyone who knows how to write a good one-act play need not fear that he must have extra special-talent for writing for that new and exciting medium: television.

They tell you that from the moment a play starts on the television screen, the story must have the power to hold the audience spellbound to the very end. This is nothing new to a good playwright.

We were dealing with this very principle all along in "Point of Attack." How to generate interest and conflict in television is exactly the same as in a good play.

The author of television shows need not worry about camera angles or any other peculiarities of a production.

The difference between a one-act play and half-hour television show is that while the one-acter will preferably use one scene, a television show prefers three or four scenes, and it is permissible to alternate them as many times as the play demands it. And, of course, television producers also prefer as few characters as possible.

The peculiarity of a television typewritten *script* is that it should be written to one half of the page instead of utilizing the whole page.

Here is the beginning of a television show that two of my students have written, which was produced on "Danger," Station C.B.S.

## THE ANNIVERSARY

A Play for Television
by
Evelyn Cornell
and
John T. Chapman

## CHARACTERS:

Katharine McCloud
Alan McCloud
Charlie Dean
Mrs. Bryce
Josef Kucharski
The Prosecuting Attorney
The Judge
A Delivery Boy

## SCENE:

The McClouds' renovated farmhouse in Connecticut.

[ 192 ]

The front door has a heavy glass panel and opens into a wide central hallway which has double doors leading at the left into a dining room and other doors at the right leading into the living room.

Stairs in the hall lead to the second floor. A door to the kitchen is in the dining room. The bedroom and the courtroom may be small insets.

It is an early spring day.

(MRS. BRYCE ENTERS DINING ROOM FROM KITCHEN, CARRYING COFFEE SERVICE WHICH SHE TAKES TO SIDEBOARD. SHE IS FORTYISH, Typically rural New England. At a SOUND IN HALL SHE TURNS TO DOUBLE DOORS AS ALAN McCLOUD ENTERS, TOSSING HAT, TOPCOAT AND BRIEFCASE ONTO CHAIR. HE IS ABOUT 35, THIN AND HARASSED - LOOKING,

DECIDEDLY IRRITABLE
AT THE MOMENT.)

MRS. BRYCE:
Good morning, Mr. Mc-
Cloud.

ALAN:
Morning, Mrs. Bryce. Is coffee ready?

MRS. BRYCE:
Yes, sir. Will you be having
eggs?

ALAN:
(SITS AT TABLE)
I'm afraid there isn't time,
Mrs. Bryce. I have to take
the early train into town.
Court opens this morning
and this case I've been work-
ing on is first on the
docket . . .
(SHE POURS COFFEE. HE
PUTS HIS FACE INTO
HIS HANDS, STRAIGHT-
ENS AS SHE BRINGS CUP)
Let's see . . . Thursday . . . I
wonder if you'd mind not
taking your afternoon off to-
day? (SHE LOOKS AT
HIM, PREPARED TO OB-
JECT) Mrs. McCloud is . . .
she hasn't been very well and

has been having trouble
sleeping . . .

MRS. BRYCE:
Well . . . if the poor dear is
sick, maybe I should call the
doctor . . .

ALAN:
Oh, it isn't . . . she isn't really
ill! (GLANCES AT HER,
SHE SEEMS TO BE WAIT-
ING FOR MORE. HE
PUTS DOWN CUP)
The fact is . . . she's not her-
self, hasn't been for some
time . . . (PAUSE)

MRS. BRYCE:
(UNCOMFORTABLY)
Yes, sir . . . she has been a bit
strange . . .

ALAN:
(AFTER A MOMENT)
Yes . . . she shouldn't be left
alone.

MRS. BRYCE:
I've made plans for today . . .

ALAN:
(NOT LISTENING)
But it'll pass . . . she'll be all
right, I'm sure . . . after to-
day . . . (SUDDENLY RE-
MEMBERS MRS. B.) Oh . . .

I'm sorry . . . you were saying . . . ?

MRS. BRYCE:
I say I have plans for today. Couldn't somebody else . . .

ALAN:
There's nobody else. I have to be at court and her mother . . . (GESTURES IMPATIENTLY) Her mother is in Florida. . . . Please . . . it would mean a lot to me. If you promise not to leave her . . . not once, today . . . I'll make it worth your while . . .

MRS. BRYCE:
(SLOWLY)
All right . . . I'll stay. Shall I take her breakfast up?

ALAN:
(FINISHING COFFEE)
No, don't disturb her . . . she only dropped off about an hour ago. (RISES, TAKES COAT, ETC.) All that's required is that someone *be* here. If . . . anything should happen you can leave word at the District Attorney's office. Thank you for staying, Mrs. Bryce . . .

(SHE NODS: HE GOES TO HALL. AS HE NEARS FRONT DOOR, A DOOR BANGS UPSTAIRS, HE GLANCES UP AS KATHARINE HURRIES DOWNSTAIRS. SHE IS ABOUT 30, NORMALLY A WOMAN OF MUCH CHARM. SHE WEARS HER NIGHTGOWN. HOLDS ROBE ABOUT HER, IS VERY AGITATED)

KATHARINE:
(CALLING)
Alan! Alan, wait!

ALAN:
(GRABS HER)
Katharine! I thought you were asleep!

KATHARINE:
(CLINGING TO HIM)
You were leaving! You were going away without a single thought for me!

ALAN:
That isn't true, Katharine! I *have* to go into town! This case . . . is . . .

KATHARINE:
But you mustn't! How can

you be so cruel to me? Think what I've been through, every day worse than the last and all of them building up to this! You *can't* leave me! It's April 6th, Alan! It's . . .

ALAN:
(STERNLY)
Stop thinking about it, Katharine!

KATHARINE:
(FIERCELY)
How can I? I'm going with you!

ALAN:
(SHAKES HER)
That's impossible! Now, I want you to go upstairs and sleep! Take some of those pills . . .

KATHARINE:
It doesn't do any good! As soon as I close my eyes I see him, his face, his finger pointing! I hear him . . .

ALAN:
(ANGRILY)
Katharine!
(SHE DRAWS AWAY, FRIGHTENED AT HIS VOICE)

ALAN:

I don't want to hear about it again! Is it your intention to deliberately distract me when I'm doing difficult work?

KATHARINE:

Oh, no, Alan . . . I'd never do such a thing! But . . . I've been so frightened!

ALAN:

(STILL ANGRY)

And why? Because some insane criminal makes an absurd threat against you! You must get this hysterical nonsense out of your head! (SHE GIVES A LITTLE CRY, TURNS AWAY, HE FOLLOWS)

ALAN:

That man is dead, Katharine! He has been for a whole year!

KATHARINE:

But he promised revenge, Alan . . . and he promised it for today! (SHE TURNS BACK, HER VOICE RISING) I remember just how he looked! It was horrible, he was almost smiling! *Do* we know he's dead? We didn't see him die! (GOES TO HIM, GRABS HIS ARMS) He meant it, I know he meant it! Even if he's dead, he has a family . . . friends who . . .

ALAN:

Don't be a fool, Katharine! You are perfectly safe! Mrs. Bryce will stay till . . .

KATHARINE:

(LOOKS AT HIM) Mrs. Bryce? But I don't want her! What do we know about her? She may be . . .

ALAN:

(VIOLENTLY) Stop it! We've been through this kind of scene a hundred times and I'm sick of humoring you! (SHE RECOILS AS IF HE HAD STRUCK HER) You are to go upstairs *now* and get some rest before you make yourself really ill! I'll expect to find you behaving like a rational human being by the time I'm home.

You'll notice that the play starts with something sinister brewing in the air. Foreshadowing conflict. Suspense mounts at every passing moment, and you find yourself interested and you want to know what's going to happen to this woman in the story. All plays should start in the middle of the middle. The exception is a three-act play, where you have more time, but nevertheless—the principle is the same—suspense, the foreshadowing conflict, should hover like a dark shadow over everything from the very beginning.

A television typewritten script usually runs from forty to fifty *half pages*. Notice that the instructions are all typed in capitals.

No, you need not be afraid of television writing if you first master the principles of good writing.

# Epilogue

Let me suppose that you finished writing a very good play. Even your severest critic, your wife, and all of your best friends are raving about it. They call it a gem and they're sure if it is produced it'll be a smash hit. Of course you're very happy to hear all this and you proceed to type up six good copies for your agent. No doubt your agent is going to like it enormously, only he'll have some slight suggestions for improving your piece.

Very well. It is your first play and you're very happy that he, the agent, being a big shot and all that, not only thinks it is worth while to sit down and read it, but to top it all, he is willing to advise you how to improve on it. Oh baby, what a break!

In your great happiness you promise everything—only your heart jumps up into your throat when you hear that the central character, which is the pivotal character, must be the antagonist, because he is a man, good-looking, and much easier to save. You'd better listen. You listen, all right, and you're ready to go home and rewrite your play, but your agent calls you back. He's not finished yet. He just started to talk. Listen: The elopement is all out. It is better if she's raped first by the protagonist just a day before her marriage. She is shattered, of course, who wouldn't be, but the audience will lap it up.

Remember, she can't tell Bob about the incident and she simply pines away, carrying that terrible secret in her heart because she's honest and can't live in sin, but if she opens her big mouth, her husband, Bob, that is, is going to kill that bastard, whose name is Eddy, and it's absolutely unbelievable, but true, that he's Gertrude's uncle.

Who's Gertrude? you ask. The bride. You say that this is not your play? Of course not, but look at the improvement. That rape business is going to slay them. If you try to protest, as I imagine you will, he'll tell you, being very much hurt, that he's supposed to know, because he's in this business over thirty years. He's the representative of you know whom? Shaw, O'Neill, Behrman, Barry, Miller. . . . Now are you impressed? You'd better be! You pull in your tail and go home to write your agent's play. Because now it is his and no more yours. But you're going to write it, nevertheless, because he's sure to sell it, and you want your play to be sold. I don't blame you.

He said he's going to sell it and he's supposed to know, because—shall I remind you again?—he's in the business over thirty years.

O.K. You've rewritten your play exactly as your wonderful agent had told you and you know what, he likes it too. Why not, after all it is his play.

Shall I make it short? O.K. A producer likes it very much, but he wouldn't mind a little change here and there. Not much, mind you, and even your all-knowing agent agrees with him this time. You see, that uncle of hers should have raped her nine months ago and not the day before the wedding and she kept it a secret, the little dope, and just the day before the marriage—now watch this—it'll murder them. Honest it will. Listen, she'll give birth to a little girl in her room while she's all alone, with curly blonde hair and blue eyes—the baby, that is—but she can't keep it, because that would ruin her marriage —so she throws it down the incinerator. The audience would gasp in delight because they, the audience, love brutal love, and brutal everything. It's going to be a real smash! A classic, your producer assures you.

What can you say? Isn't he a producer? He is! Isn't he in the business over thirty-five years? You have to admit he is! Didn't he produce twenty-nine total failures against three successes in these thirty-five years? Bet your life he did! Then what are you waiting for? So go home and write it as the advice of your best friend on earth, your agent.

Shall I tell you what you're going to do? You'll go home and write it, although you fell sick in your stomach. Yes, I know, you need money, you want to see your name in big electric lights, and all the rest. You'll put in four more months and then bring it back to the producer. He'll keep it for two months. You become impatient, you call him on the phone. "Yes, yes," he says. "I am going to read it and for Pete's sake, don't clang that phone every day," says the big potentate. Do you think he has nothing else to do only to read your play?

"Yeah, yeah," you stammer, and apologize, and hang up. A week later you try again. The big stinker is out in the country this time and his blond bombshell informs you that he won't be back before Christmas. How about the play? What play? she inquires, bored. *The Red Pajama,* you say. The title originally was *Black Symphony,* but no one liked it. The glamour girl doesn't know a thing about your play, but she'll ask when the big jerk comes back by Christmas.

You grit your teeth and wait. He comes back, all right, but gives you the cold shoulder. Yeah, he read *The Red Pajama* he says; but it hasn't what it takes. What does that mean? It means he doesn't want it. So what are you going to do? Your wonderful agent gives it to another big producer. He is really very big, he's in the business over forty-seven years. He likes the play all right, but. . . .

And the old song starts all over again. "Just a little change," he says, and he tells you about what he'd like to see in your play. It'll be a classic if you'll do it his way. Should you do it?

I say, No! Don't you dare to listen to your wonderful agent, or the oldest or most influential and most successful producer. They express their individual opinions. Out of one hundred plays produced, ninety-four are total failures. The only remedy against them is that *you must know your business better than they do.*

If you'll listen to everyone, you'll be like a weather vane, and in the end they'll drive you insane.

The wise thing to do is, first, if a producer likes your play, to let him sign a contract, which goes through the capable hands of the "Dramatist Guild." They'll advise you what are your rights and what are the producer's rights. But what is more important than anything else is that you must know your own mind. You must know what kind of play you wrote. Don't let yourself be pushed around. The greater the producer is, the greater and more numerous the failures he has made in his lifetime. He has no formula for success. You and only you must know whether you have written a good play or not. Character is the foundation of all writing. Tear him apart. I mean your character. Show us the working of his mind in distress. But, for the grace of God, any one of us might be that man. Remember, people are interested in others, especially when they're in trouble, and they love to watch as the characters solve their problems or die defeated.

Remember conflict. Conflict is the essence of life. When you have finished your play and managed to put in all the elements as I presented them in "Basic Principles of Writing," it still means nothing without living human beings in it.

Yes, I am sure there are still a few more good agents and producers at large. But they are as rare as buffaloes roaming the prairies. Listen to the producer *if he wants to buy* your play—but don't change a line before he signs your contract. And even then, rewrite only what *you think* will *improve* your play. The revised script should be according to your own idea and you should take all the responsibility for all the changes made.

### GOOD LUCK TO YOU!

# Glossary of
# T.V. Terms

| | |
|---|---|
| B.C.U.: | Abbreviation for Big Close-up. |
| Bridge: | A connecting link between one scene or action and another. Most usually a term in nondramatic writing; the term transition is used in dramatic writing. |
| Close-up: | Camera concentration on an object or a person. With a person the frame would be entirely filled by the head and shoulders. |
| Cold: | Music, sound, or voices heard alone or in clear. |
| Cross-fade: | To fade out one picture and to fade in another. Audio—to fade out one sound and to fade in another. |
| Cut: | To stop an action, cameras, etc. |
| Cut to: | To switch from one camera to another—hence, one picture to another. |
| Dissolve: | To fade out one picture as another picture simultaneously is faded in. |
| Dissolve in: | To fade in a new picture. |
| Dissolve out: | To fade out a picture. Both these terms indicative of the dissolve. |
| Direct Cut: | An abrupt visual transition from the image of one camera to the image of another. |
| Dolly to: | Motion by a camera as it moves toward or away from an object. |
| Dolly in: | To move the camera toward an object or person. |

| | |
|---|---|
| Dolly out: | To move the camera back from an object. |
| Fade in: | Video—a picture gradually appears on a dark screen. Audio—to bring up, gradually, the volume of a voice, a sound, or music. |
| Fade out: | Video—a picture gradually fades from full brightness until the screen is dark. Audio—to diminish the volume of a sound until it is no longer audible. |
| Film Clip: | Film inserted into a live telecast. |
| Frame: | What the camera sees from a fixed position. |
| Full Back: | To dolly out from a close-up. |
| Long Shot: | A shot which includes the foreground as well as the background. |
| In: | Music comes in. |
| In Clear: | The same as cold. |
| Over Frame: | The speaker or the source of the sound is not visible in the frame of the picture. |
| Panning: | To begin a shot at one position and to move to another position without a break. |
| Sneak: | To bring in music, sound, or voices at an extremely low level of volume. |
| Sustain: | Keep the music going. |
| Under: | Music goes on under dialogue or narration. |
| Back with Music: | Words spoken over musical background. |
| Down: | The volume of the music is lowered. |
| Music in B.G.: | Music in the background. |
| Over Music: | Words spoken over musical background. |
| Out: | The music stops. |
| Sting: | To punctuate with a sudden musical phrase or chord. |
| Up: | The volume of the music is raised. |